MODERN SALADS

200 PERFECT STARTERS, MAINS AND DESSERTS

Produced by ACP Books
Printed by Bookbuilders, China.
Published by ACP Magazines Ltd, 54 Park Street, Sydney, NSW 2000 (GPO Box 4088, Sydney, NSW 2001),
phone (02) 9282 8618, fax (02) 9267 9438, www.acpbooks.com.au
AUSTRALIA: Distributed by Network Services, GPO Box 4088, Sydney, NSW 2001, phone (02) 9282 8777, fax (02) 9264 3278.
UNITED KINGDOM: Distributed by Australian Consolidated Press (UK), Moulton Park Business Centre, Red House Road,
Moulton Park, Northampton, NN3 6AQ, phone (01604) 497 531, fax (01604) 497 533, acpukltd@aol.com
CANADA: Distributed by Whitecap Books Ltd, 351 Lynn Avenue, North Vancouver, BC, V7J 2C4,
phone (604) 980 9852, fax (604) 980 8197, customerservice@whitecap.ca www.whitecap.ca
NEW ZEALAND: Distributed by Southern Publishers Group, 44 New North Road, Eden Terrace, Auckland
phone (649) 309 6930, fax (649) 309 6170, hub@spg.co.nz
Australian Gourmet Traveller Modern Salads.
Includes index.
ISBN-13 978-1-86396-423-4.
ISBN-10 1 86396 423 1.
1. Salads. I. Title: Australian Gourmet Traveller.
641.83
© ACP Magazines Ltd 2005
ABN 18 053 273 546
First published 2005. Reprinted 2006.
Front cover: Goat's cheese, pear and hazelnut salad with bitter leaves; see recipe on page 46.

AUSTRALIAN GOURMET TRAVELLER
Group publisher Phil Scott
Associate publisher Marijcke Thomson
Editorial director Andy Harris
Creative director Emma Ross
Editor Anthea Loucas

Photographer Brett Stevens
Stylists Yael Grinham, Jane Hann, Kate Nixon
(chapter openers)
Food preparation Julie Ballard, Sally Lewis,
Hannah Dodds
Feature writers Kathleen Gandy, Meg Thomason

ACP BOOKS
Editorial director Susan Tomnay
Creative director Hieu Chi Nguyen
Editors Klay Lamprell, Annette Madjarian
Designer Caryl Wiggins
Sales director Brian Cearnes
Marketing manager Bridget Cody
Production manager Cedric Taylor
Rights enquiries Laura Bamford, Director ACP Books
lbamford@acpmedia.co.uk
Chief executive officer Ian law
Group publisher Pat Ingram
General manager Christine Whiston

RECIPE CONTRIBUTORS
**Sara Backhouse; Jane Charlton; Bronwen Clark;
Rodney Dunn; Sue Fairlie-Cuninghame;
Lisa Featherby; Kathleen Gandy; Fiona Hammond;
Jane Hann; Andy Harris; Leanne Kitchen;
Lynne Mullins; Christine Osmond; Kathy Snowball;
Kate Tait; Sophia Young.**

THANKS TO THESE STOCKISTS AND SUPPLIERS
Accoutrement, phone (02) 9969 1031
All Hand Made, phone (02) 9386 4099
Anvoy Marketing, phone (02) 9682 1395
Bed Bath N' Table, phone (03) 9387 3322
Cloth, phone (02) 9326 7755
Design 4 Space, phone (02) 9555 8308
Design Mode, phone (02) 9998 8200
Duck Egg Blue, phone (02) 9810 8855
Essential Ingredient, phone (02) 9550 5477
Food Stuff, Mona Vale, phone (02) 9999 3033
Funkis Swedish Forms, phone (02) 9365 0573
IKEA, phone (02) 9313 6400
Le Forge, phone (02) 9516 3888
Legnoart, phone (02) 9363 2777
MUD Australia, phone (02) 9699 7600
New Direction Imports, phone (02) 9667 3299
No Chintz, phone (02) 9318 2080
Orson & Blake, phone (02) 9326 1155
Papaya, phone (02) 9386 9980
Prime Quality Meats, phone (02) 9958 2186
Quarella, phone 1800 782 789
Ripe Grocer, phone (02) 9999 6899
Simon Johnson, phone (02) 9319 6122
Space Furniture, phone (02) 9667 8200
Spence & Lyda, phone (02) 9212 6747
The Art of Wine & Food, phone (02) 9363 2817
The Bay Tree, phone (02) 9328 1101
Tomkin Australia, phone (02) 9319 2993
Top 3 By Design, phone (02) 9906 4433

AUSTRALIAN GOURMET TRAVELLER

MODERN SALADS
200 PERFECT STARTERS, MAINS AND DESSERTS

acp books

contents

what is a salad?

My first memory of salad is as part of the ritual of Sunday lunch at home in England.

My mother used to prepare a typical roast of beef or chicken with vegetables accompanied by a green salad, served in a well-used, large cherrywood bowl. From an early age, I learnt how to pick a variety of salad greens and herbs from our vegetable garden before preparing the dressing in the bowl. This was always under precise instruction* and, depending on what I had picked, we sometimes used walnut oil instead of olive oil and often experimented with a variety of vinegars.

As a more rebellious teenager, I would subtract or add ingredients with varying degrees of success – rubbing too much garlic around the bowl when that was all the vogue in the late 1970s and having a more serious relapse when I tried to spice up our lives with a can of pickled green peppercorns I'd found in the kitchen pantry. My mother favoured the French model of mesclun salad [usually a mixture of rocket, dandelion, frisée, lamb's lettuce, chicory, watercress and a couple of types of lettuce] and the best part of a meal was always the transference of this lightly dressed mix of leaves onto our plates where they combined with the gravy juices from the Sunday roast. It's still very much a part of our family tradition and, I've since learnt, most gatherings around France.

So what is a salad exactly? In its most basic, perhaps best incarnation, it's some lettuce simply dressed with vinaigrette, or a composed salad [a mixture of leaves with cold meats, fish or eggs]. For some, it might be a warm mixture of lightly steamed vegetables with a herb dressing or a combination of ingredients that are chopped or shredded or sliced and tossed together with a creamy sauce. The truth is, a salad can be anything you want it to be.

Salads are integral in the antipasti, tapas and mezze consumed daily around the Mediterranean. Modern Greeks have a repertoire of four seasonal salads – a horiatiki summer salad of tomatoes, cucumber, onions and feta; a spring salad of shredded cos, spring onions and dill; a winter salad of shredded cabbage and carrot; and horta [boiled greens such as amaranth, mustard, nettles or pea shoots], dressed with extra-virgin olive oil and lemon juice and served year round. In Italy and Spain, the tomato reigns supreme, although they also have a love of wild herbs and greens and incorporate grilled vegetables, citrus fruits and bread in their salads.

Rustic peasant salads such as panzanella from Tuscany and fattoush from the Middle East are fashionable in many restaurants and cafes. They began as thrifty ways to bulk out salad ingredients with stale bread to create a sustaining meal. The Tuscan farm labourer would be bemused indeed if he saw the number of ways panzanella is described on menus today, and the prices being charged for this essentially humble dish of stale bread, tomatoes, onion, cucumber, basil, olive oil and vinegar.

Bread is often used as a wrap around salads in the Middle East, especially in Israel, Syria and Lebanon. Salad, however, is the ebullient, overflowing garnish that you add yourself to a felafel sandwich at street stalls and the choices always include tabbouleh, tomatoes, lettuce, eggplant, pickled turnips, cucumbers and spicy condiments such as sumac, Aleppo pepper and hot chilli sauces. For the Maghreb countries, it's a colourful collection of raw or cooked vegetable and pulse salads, dressed with olive or argan oil, cumin and coriander, and eaten at the beginning of a meal.

In Asia, the Japanese count aemono and sunomono [dishes of vegetables and seafood pickled with vinegar and more complex dressings] as salads. In Cambodia and Vietnam, it's the leaves, herbs and pickled vegetables known as xalach dia that are always on the table and used as a palate refresher between courses or added to pho soups.

Americans traditionally think of salad as an appetiser, although millions of office workers in US cities are now addicted to the daily ritual of takeaway lunch at the substantial make-your-own salad bars in restaurants and on street corners. No wonder lettuce is the second most popular vegetable after potatoes. The acerbic food writer Jeffrey Steingarten said, "Adults who require a salad at every meal are like obsessed little children who will eat nothing but frozen pizza or canned ravioli for months on end. They tuck into the dreariest salad simply because it is raw and green."

Four perennially popular American dishes are: wilted spinach and bacon salad; Waldorf salad, which dates from 1896; Caesar salad; and Cobb salad, created by Robert Cobb for the Hollywood stars who frequented the Brown Derby restaurant in Los Angeles. The land that brought us these salads has also left us with the legacy of iceberg lettuce. Taking its name from the crushed ice used in its transportation on the railroads in the 1920s, this crisphead lettuce has played an important role in lettuce lore and has recently made a comeback, generally served in wedges with blue cheese or anchovy dressing.

For my money, the French still create some of the best salads in the world. Go to any classic Parisian brasserie for a salade frisée aux lardons or a pavement cafe for salade Niçoise, both preferably with a Poilane baguette and a glass of chilled Loire white, to understand why these salads make such comforting food. Better still, visit the Conard family stand at the Sunday organic market on the Boulevard Raspail in the 6th arrondissement. You can't miss the wealthy Left Bankers queuing for its impressive display of baskets filled with freshly picked salad greens and herbs, all about to be tossed into salad bowls on classic French tables.

Salad-making inventiveness started long before the French, however. The ancient Greek hedonist philosopher Aristoxenus sprinkled the lettuces in his garden with wine and honey every evening. The next day at dawn, he would pick them and eat them with their ready-made dressing. In those times, lettuce varieties were headless and stalky with leaves that grew outwards like a cardoon, some so tall that they were used as gates to protect vegetable gardens. They were mostly eaten raw with salt [the word salad is derived from the Latin for salt, sal, a derivation of this very practice] although in Roman times, the noted gourmand Apicius records a spicy cheese, honey, wine, herb and garum dressing in his cookbook. The soporific effects of lettuce were well known to both the ancient Greeks and Romans who preferred to serve it at the end of a meal, although by the time of the Emperor Domitian it was served at the beginning of imperial feasts to cruelly test his subject's alertness. The Roman poet Martial even echoes Jeffrey Steingarten's views in an epigram: "Lettuce once closed the dinners of our ancestors; Tell me, why today does it open ours?"

By medieval times, lettuces were mostly confined to monastic gardens and not widely eaten, although wild leaves and herbs [many favoured in mesclun mixes today] such as purslane, lamb's lettuce, cresses, rocket, chickweed, nettles, parsley, sage and mint were used in salads dressed with olive oil, vinegar and salt. Flowers, such as dandelions, daisies, alexanders, primroses, borage and nasturtium, were added. With the rise of market gardens in Europe in the 17th century, new varieties of lettuce became a favoured salad ingredient. John Evelyn's *Acetaria – A discourse of Sallets* [1699] is the first book devoted to the art of salad making.

Despite Evelyn's admirable recipes, the English were not known for the quality of their salads. The Chevalier d'Albignac, who fled to England during the French revolution, was so disgusted by the English 'boiled' salad dressings, that he started a business making salads for London's aristocrats. At mealtimes he drove around London in his open carriage, calling at the various households where he had been summoned and set about making salads. His servant carried a mahogany case containing all the ingredients for his dressings: oils, vinegars, caviar, truffles and anchovies. He became widely known and started a successful sideline selling his salad dressing cases stocked with ingredients, enabling him to eventually buy a chateau in Limousin when he returned to France.

In recent years, one of the biggest changes in our eating habits is that we now eat salads as a main course without feeling we've been deprived of the usual meat and three veg. We eat them warm or cold in winter as well as in summer. Seafood salads, warm chicken and game-bird salads, beef and lamb salads; no longer are salads the province of the dieting brigade or ladies who lunch – they've become everyone's favourite food. The recipes in this book, *Modern Salads*, reflect the diversity on offer in our multicultural society.

A food for all occasions, the salad remains one of the most versatile and imaginative dishes in the cook's repertoire. Whatever your ideas of a salad might be, once you start improvising with changing seasonal ingredients, adding leftovers or using new cooking fashions to colour your salad moods, the culinary adventure really begins.

Andy Harris

Andy Harris, Editorial Director, Australian Gourmet Traveller

✱ My mother's classic salad dressing combines 1 tsp sugar, ½ tbsp English mustard powder, 4 tbsp olive oil, 2 tbsp white wine vinegar, sea salt and black pepper. Sometimes she substitutes lemon juice for the vinegar and adds some finely chopped herbs.

oils, vinegars & mustards

A good dressing is the soul of a salad, and oils, vinegars and mustards are the major players. These essential ingredients are available in an ever-increasing variety, sometimes at startling prices, so it pays to know something about them.

Oil used for salads should be cold-pressed, meaning that it has been extracted without heat or chemicals and retains its full, natural flavour. Price does, in general, reflect quality, so long as you avoid fancy packaging. The fresher an oil is, the better, so buy it in quantities that you will use within a month or two.

Fine vinegar is made from good wine [or cider, for cider vinegar] inoculated with a 'vinegar mother' [the clumped-together, naturally occurring bacteria which causes fermentation] and aged slowly in wood. Inexpensive commercial vinegars use cheaper ingredients and speed up the process to days rather than months or years, so their flavour is one-dimensional, rather than subtle and complex.

Different regions of the world prefer different styles of mustards. However, all good mustards are distinguished by a clean taste, and the best have a subtle, underlying balance of flavours.

oils

NUT OILS [1, 7, 8]

Walnut oil [1] and hazelnut oil [8] are cold-pressed from either raw or roasted nuts – the former giving a deeper flavour, the latter a more delicate one. Cold-pressed nut oils are best used in cold dishes, as heat destroys their delicate flavour. They bring a rich quality to a salad, especially if a few of the appropriate nuts are added, whole or chopped. These oils are expensive and do not keep well; buy them in small quantities, store tightly sealed in the refrigerator and use within a few months. Refrigerated nut oils congeal, so bring them to room temperature before using.

Argan oil [7], from the nuts of the argan tree in Morocco, has come to the attention of Australian chefs only recently, though it has been prized for centuries in its homeland. It is not recommended for cooking but is suggested as a flavoursome dressing on hot foods and salads.

Peanut oil is highly regarded by the chefs of many countries because it performs well at high temperatures and it is almost invariably refined to the point of having no distinct smell or taste – an attribute that particularly suits Asian chefs, who like to flavour oil themselves by heating it with ginger, garlic or green onion before starting to cook. It keeps well in an airtight bottle away from light and heat.

GRAPESEED OIL [2]

This pale, golden, slightly aromatic oil, a by-product of the wine industry, is the popular choice in France and Italy as a light and mild-tasting alternative to olive oil. It is mainly used for gentle frying and for salads.

SESAME OIL [3]

Strongly flavoured oil of toasted sesame seeds. Widely used in Asian cooking.

EXTRA-VIRGIN OLIVE OIL [4], OLIVE OIL [5]

Virgin olive oil comes from the first cold pressing of the olives. It has not been processed or refined in any way, and is low in acid content because it has been pressed from fresh, sound fruit at the correct point of ripeness. Virgin olive oil may be golden or greenish in colour.

Extra-virgin olive oil is virgin oil that is very low in acid content – no more than one per cent – and has been judged by a panel of accredited experts to be of the finest flavour and aroma. The flavours of extra-virgin olive oils vary considerably, from strong and fruity to delicate, and display such individual characteristics as pungency, a touch of bitterness or pepperiness. These are all desirable qualities provided they are present in moderation and in balance with other flavour components.

Taste carefully when using these oils for mayonnaise or other salad dressings – some olive oils are quite assertive and you may wish to soften the flavour with a milder oil.

Lesser olive oils may come entirely from subsequent pressings or may be a mixture of first and later pressings. As multiple pressings extract substances that give a harsh flavour to the oil, it has to be refined with chemicals to remove these and, along with them, some of the desirable flavour nuances. Olive oils labelled 'light' have been processed to remove most of the flavour.

CITRUS-PRESSED OILS [6]

The wonderful aroma of fresh oranges or lemons is derived from the oil contained in the zest – the thin, coloured, outer layer of the skins. The zest is added to olive oil at the pressing stage. Many recipes call for grated zest as an ingredient, but it is good to have that matchless fragrance and flavour on hand in the convenient form of oil pressed from lemon or orange skins.

CANOLA OIL

Some years ago, the Canadian oil industry developed a new, healthier oil from rape-seed oil and named it canola [derived from the words 'Canadian oil']. The product and name have spread to numerous countries, including Australia, and it is now one of the most popular all-purpose oils. It can be used as a light salad oil or for any kind of cooking as it performs well at high temperatures. Canola oil will keep for up to a year in an airtight bottle away from heat or light.

1 Huile de noix J. Leblanc 25 CL

2 Huile de

3

4 L'ORIGINALE Olio E Vergine estratto a

5

6 COLONNA® ARANCIO EXTRA-VIRGIN OLIVE OIL AND NATURAL ZEST OF ORANGES produced by Principessa Marina Colonna Estate bottled at Bosco Pontoni Località San Martino in Pensilis Best before: see date on seal PRODUCT OF ITALY NET. 0.25 l. e 8.45 fl. oz.

7 MAS Argan 250 ml

8

vinegars

SHERRY VINEGAR [1]

This fine vinegar uses oloroso [medium-sweet] sherry as the base wine, and is aged in sherry casks. The best comes from Jerez in Spain, also the home of the finest sherries, and is aged by the same solera system as the sherries – a complex process of gradually blending younger and increasingly older vinegars, giving great depth and complexity to the final product.

RASPBERRY VINEGAR [2]

Fruit, herb or spiced vinegar is made by steeping the chosen flavouring ingredients in white or red wine vinegar for 24 hours or more, then filtering. Raspberry vinegar, one of the most popular flavours, is delicious in salad dressings or sprinkled sparingly on poached fruit.

BALSAMIC VINEGAR [3]

The home of balsamic vinegar is Modena and the surrounding area in Italy. All true balsamics still come from there, so look for Modena on the label. True balsamics have been barrel-aged, so the label should also state this. The top rank of balsamics is labelled 'traditionale', often with a maker's registration number. They have been made with prized, heirloom vinegar mothers, and aged in a succession of small barrels of different woods over many years, giving them their hallmark colour and deep, sharp/sweet complexity. These can cost hundreds of dollars for a small bottle. Most balsamic vinegars, however, are classified as commercial, are aged for shorter periods in much larger barrels, and have caramel and other ingredients added.

CIDER VINEGAR [4]

The best cider vinegar is made from good hard cider aged in wood, and has a delicate underlying apple note. It is sharper than wine vinegar but not as sharp as malt vinegar. Cider vinegar is used for pickling fruit and is especially good in a dressing for a salad containing apples or pears.

**CHARDONNAY VINEGAR [5],
CABERNET SAUVIGNON VINEGAR [7]**

These vinegars are made from the wines for which they are named. The implication of such specific naming is that the base wines were quality examples of their kind, and so the vinegar possesses the same fine characters.

RICE VINEGAR [6]

Chinese and Japanese vinegars are less acidic than Western ones, and Thai vinegar is milder still. They are made from rice wine or sake and have a subtle tang with a hint of sweetness. They are used for sushi, sweet-and-sour dishes, dipping sauces and salads.

CHAMPAGNE VINEGAR [8]

This delicate vinegar is the result of a process activated when the second, in-bottle fermentation of Champagne [the one that produces the bubbles] is complete. The bottleneck is frozen and uncapped, and then the spent yeast cells are expelled in a plug of frozen wine. This wine, filtered, is used as the base wine for delicate Champagne vinegar.

MALT VINEGAR

Malt vinegar used to be called alegar, a more appropriate name for this vinegar which is made from an unhopped type of beer. The dark colour and malty taste may be too strong for raw salad vegetables but is particularly useful for pickling watery vegetables.

mustards

DIJON MUSTARD [1]

Dijon in Burgundy has been famous for mustard since Roman times. The term moutarde de Dijon is an appellation contrôlée which may be used only for mustard made by the Dijon method, for which the soaked, ground and sieved mustard seed is mixed with wine, vinegar or verjuice, salt and spices and matured for about a week before being bottled. Dijon mustards may be mild or strong. They are considered the aristocrats of mustards, having a clean taste with a delicate acid edge and subtle undertone. If a recipe calls for mustard without any further specification, use Dijon.

HERB MUSTARD, HONEY MUSTARD, HONEY SPICED MUSTARD [2]

Tarragon, thyme, horseradish or other herbs can be chopped and added to mixed mustard to flavour it. Other flavouring ingredients are green peppercorns, garlic, or a little honey, with or without spices. Mixed with a little oil, flavoured mustard can be brushed on meat as a marinade.

ENGLISH MUSTARD [3]

English mustard is straightforward and hot. You can buy it ready-mixed, but freshly mixed is better and very easily made: put about half a teaspoon of mustard powder per person into a small container and gradually add cold water, stirring until you have a smooth, creamy paste. Cover and stand for 10-15 minutes to allow the flavour to develop. Don't use hot water or vinegar, which will make the mustard milder but bitter. Mustard powder will remain fresh and potent for about a year, provided it is kept dry and stored away from heat.

VIOLET MUSTARD [4]

Made by boiling down black grapes, then straining and mixing the purple liquid with mustard powder. The resulting mustard is violet-coloured and has a rich wine flavour. It is excellent on roast beef or steak.

SEEDED MUSTARD, MEAUX MUSTARD [5]

Seeded mustards have a speckled appearance and grainy texture from a mixture of ground and whole seeds. They are usually blended to be a little sharper than smooth mustards. The most famous is Meaux mustard, originally made by the monks at Meaux, a town near Paris. The formula was given to the Pommery family, of Champagne fame, in the 18th century, and Pommery moutarde de Meaux is still considered to be the best of the seeded mustards. It is fairly strong, with a blend of pleasantly musty, hot and sharp notes.

MUSTARD OIL

Expressed from mustard seeds, this hot, pungent oil is suitable for salad dressings on raw crunchy vegetables, marinades and stir-fried dishes. Store in the refrigerator for up to six months.

MUSTARD SEEDS

Mustard seeds come from three members of the cabbage family: black, brown and yellow mustard. The seeds themselves are not hot, but pleasantly nutty with a mild mustard tang. The heat develops when the ground seed is mixed with water. The water reacts with the seeds' glucosides [bitter substances related to sugar] through the action of an enzyme also in the seed to develop the characteristic mustard bite. Black mustard seeds, with the highest glucoside level, are the strongest, then come the brown seeds, then the yellow. Mixing with plain cold water makes the hottest mustard, while mixing with wine, verjuice, milk or cream makes milder mustards. Fried, whole mustard seeds are widely used in Indian and Middle Eastern cookery.

SAFFRON AIOLI

CLASSIC MAYONNAISE

3 egg yolks
2 tsp Dijon mustard
150 ml olive oil
150 ml sunflower oil
1-2 tbsp lemon juice or lime juice

Assemble and measure all ingredients – as a general rule of thumb, the ratio is 100ml oil to 1 egg yolk. The simplicity of mayonnaise means that it is imperative to use the freshest ingredients possible. The oils should be combined in a bottle or a jug.

1 Place a bowl on a damp tea towel [this helps to stabilise the bowl while whisking], add egg yolks and mustard, then stir to combine.
2 Whisking continuously, gradually add combined oils to egg yolk mixture, drop by drop at first, then in a thin, steady stream, until mixture is thick and emulsified.
3 Add lemon or lime juice to taste and whisk until incorporated, then season to taste. Mayonnaise will keep, closely covered with plastic wrap or in an airtight container, in the refrigerator for up to 1 week.
Makes about 1½ cups

AIOLI

4 large cloves of garlic, coarsely chopped
3 egg yolks
300 ml olive oil

1 Place garlic and ½ tsp sea salt in a mortar and, using a pestle, pound to form a coarse paste.
2 Transfer garlic paste to a bowl, add egg yolks and stir to combine. Whisking continuously, gradually add oil, drop by drop at first, then in a thin, steady stream, until mixture is thick and emulsified. Season to taste with sea salt. Serve with roast beef, lamb or potatoes, grilled or fried fish and seafood, or poached chicken.
Makes about 2 cups

VARIATION

✽ To make saffron aïoli, soak ½ tsp saffron threads in 2 tbsp hot water for 10 minutes, then add saffron mixture to egg yolks and follow aïoli recipe above. Serve spoonfuls with gutsy seafood soups, or spread on croutons and top with sautéed scallops or prawns.
Makes about 2 cups

leaves

The simplest of all salads – no more than leaves and dressing – is probably the most useful. It's the kind you'll make again and again to go with a grill or roast, with fish, pasta and scores of other hot dishes, and, of course, with cold meats, seafood and cheese. Many of the salads here would work perfectly as courses in their own right – either as a first course or as a separate course served, in the French manner, after the main course.

Easy as it is, a first-class green salad still calls for care in the making. The greens must be young and fresh, and carefully trimmed, washed, dried and crisped in the refrigerator. Dressing ingredients must be the best – a quality oil [extra-virgin olive, or a fine nut oil] and good wine vinegar or fresh lemon juice. While the dressing may be made ahead and just given a final whisk when it is wanted, the salad should be assembled and dressed at the last moment before it goes to the table so that it looks beautifully light and fresh. One point to remember – add only about half the dressing at first to a salad to be tossed, then add more while you're tossing, but stop as soon as every leaf is glistening. Too much dressing makes for a heavy, settled look rather than the delightfully bouffant one you're aiming for.

salad leaves

RADICCHIO [1]

There are many varieties of radicchio, often called after their places of origin, such as round-headed Verona or elongated Treviso. All have a refreshing yet bitter flavour and a sturdy texture which makes them suitable not only for salads, but for braising or barbecuing in wedges, or shredding over pizza before baking.

BABY ENDIVE OR FRISEE [2]

Curly endive belongs to the chicory family, which also includes radicchio and witlof, and is classified as a bitter green, although the bitterness is very mild in tender baby endive. This is usually sold as part of the mixture of baby leaves called mesclun, but it is sometimes available alone. It goes particularly well with nut oils and nuts such as walnuts or hazelnuts.

MIZUNA [3]

Of Japanese origin, mizuna is related to parsley and contributes crisp, aromatic flavour to salads, sandwiches, clear soups, tempura and delicate egg dishes. It is also used as a garnish.

LAMB'S LETTUCE OR MACHE [4]

Available in the cooler months, lamb's lettuce has a soft, velvety texture and a mild, refreshing flavour.

WITLOF [5]

Crunchy witlof tastes mild and fresh with a hint of bitterness, a little more noticeable in the red-tipped variety than in the yellow-green. Both kinds are grown in the dark to minimise bitterness by keeping the leaves white. Store in the refrigerator, wrapped, to exclude light and to prevent greening.

BABY BEET LEAVES [6], BABY SPINACH LEAVES

These pretty, flavoursome little leaves are usually mixed with others for a decorative look and varied texture. Used alone, both baby beet and baby spinach leaves are sturdy enough to take a warm dressing or to mix with substantial ingredients such as cheese, nuts or meat.

WILD ROCKET [7]

Wild rocket is stronger-flavoured than cultivated rocket because it has been grown more slowly, but has a similar rich, 'roast-beef' flavour with a peppery tang.

BUTTER LETTUCE, CORAL LETTUCE, OAK LEAF LETTUCE, MIGNONETTE

These are all members of the loose-hearted, soft-textured butterhead lettuce family. Used individually or mixed, they make the perfect light, fresh green salad. Use them within a day or two of purchase as they don't store well, and dress lightly so as not to weigh down the delicate leaves.

COS LETTUCE

Robust and well-flavoured, cos leaves are good for salads with heavy dressings or with other substantial ingredients such as egg, fish or bacon. The outer leaves of regular cos are coarse and often damaged, but baby cos, which is grown hydroponically and is about half the size of regular cos, has less wastage.

ICEBERG LETTUCE

The tight, cabbage-like structure of iceberg makes for low flavour because sunshine can't get in. Its pale, stiff leaves don't play well in tossed salad, but are good for shredding, using as cups for holding a filling such as prawns or spicy Asian meats, or serving in wedges with a mayonnaise-type dressing. Iceberg stores well.

WATERCRESS

The watercress you buy at the greengrocer's is usually mild with just a touch of pepperiness; wild-picked watercress, on the other hand, may be quite pungent. Store in the refrigerator, standing up in water with a plastic bag dropped loosely over, and use within a day or two.

salad herbs

MARJORAM [1]
Like its relative oregano, marjoram lends its warm flavour to tomato sauces and grilled or roasted lamb. It is good in stuffings for chicken or rabbit, and adds charm to a potato or green salad.

DILL [2]
Dill's anise flavour goes with fresh and smoked salmon or trout, shellfish, cucumber, beetroot, boiled potatoes, rice, vinaigrette or mayonnaise, and salad greens.

CHIVES [3]
Onion chives have tubular leaves, garlic chives have flat ones. Their fresh, mild taste is just right in many dishes where onion or garlic themselves would be too strong. Snip them into egg, fish and poultry dishes, mayonnaise, cream cheese and sauces, and scatter them over salads and soups.

THYME [4]
The savoury warmth of thyme complements most meats and is great with vegetables, from roast potatoes to sautéed eggplant. It goes in onion stuffings for poultry and rabbit or in lemon stuffings for fish, and gives a sunny character to salads.

SORREL [5]
The sharp, lemony tang of sorrel is magic with chicken, fish and veal and gives a lift to a green salad. Sorrel can also be cooked like English spinach, which it is mixed with sometimes.

FRENCH TARRAGON [6]
Be sure you're getting French, not Russian or Mexican tarragon. Check a leaf for a subtle aniseed scent and flavour, and for a slight numbing of the tongue when you taste it. Tarragon complements fish, eggs, chicken and veal and is elegant in salad dressings.

MINT [7]
Mint grows easily and adds freshness to drinks, sliced fruit and syrups. Spearmint is the one with long, smooth leaves. Its scent and flavour are clearer and stronger than those of common mint. Great with lamb, tomatoes, peas, potatoes, cucumber, yoghurt and many fruits.

CHERVIL [8]
Fragile, feathery chervil is one of the four herbs that make up the French fines herbes mixture [the others being parsley, chives and tarragon]. Its subtle anise flavour creates an elegant note in a salad.

BASIL
A cook's summer treasure, common or sweet basil is a tomato's best friend and lends its heady clove and anise perfume to salads, sauces and soups. Add leaves just before serving, tearing rather than chopping if possible.

CHAMOMILE FLOWERS
Chamomile is best known for the soothing tea made from its dried flowers and leaves. Fresh chamomile flowers have the same pleasant apple-like aroma and flavour.

CORIANDER
Coriander's unique flavour, with hints of anise, lemon and sage, is important in many Mexican, South American, Asian and Middle Eastern dishes. The leaves, stems and even roots are sometimes used.

FLAT-LEAF PARSLEY
Also known as Italian or continental parsley, flat-leaf parsley has more concentrated flavour than the curly kind. It has a special affinity with garlic and is lavishly used in Middle Eastern and Sicilian cooking.

OREGANO
The warm fragrance and flavour of oregano speak of Mediterranean cooking. Many cooks like to use it dried rather than fresh, especially in areas where fresh oregano doesn't reach the flavour intensity of that grown throughout the Mediterranean.

PURSLANE
This succulent is sometimes considered a weed, however Middle Eastern cooks value it for its lemony crunch, especially as an ingredient in the bread salad fattoush.

MIXED GREEN LEAF SALAD

4 cups [about 200g] mesclun

CLASSIC VINAIGRETTE

1 tbsp Dijon mustard

2 tbsp aged red wine vinegar

1 large clove of garlic, finely chopped

100 ml extra-virgin olive oil

1 tbsp finely chopped flat-leaf parsley

Mesclun, also called gourmet salad mix, is any combination of salad leaves. The mix depends on the source and the season. Commonly included are: lettuce, such as cos, butter, mignonette, coral, iceberg, oak leaf and lamb's lettuce [mâche]; leaves, such as watercress and other cress, baby beetroot and baby spinach; bitter leaves, such as baby endive, radicchio, witlof, wild rocket; Asian greens, such as mizuna, snow pea shoots, tatsoi; and salad herbs, such as sorrel, purslane, flat-leaf parsley, coriander, chervil, basil and mint.

1 Combine mustard, vinegar and garlic in a small bowl, season to taste, slowly pour in oil and whisk until well combined, then add parsley. Makes about ½ cup.

2 Place leaves in a large bowl, add dressing and toss to combine well.

Serves 4

VARIATIONS

∗ To create a more substantial salad, add: seafood, such as cooked, peeled king prawns, hot-smoked trout or salmon; cured meat, including prosciutto, pancetta, coppa or bresaola; leftover leg ham, roast turkey or chicken; or cheese such as crumbled feta or goat's cheese, wedges of blue cheese, semi-hard cheeses such as cheddar, or hard cheese such as shaved Parmigiano Reggiano, pecorino or grana padano. For textural contrast, visual appeal and additional flavour, try adding croutons, crisp-fried capers, caper berries, olives, semi-dried tomatoes, citrus fruit segments or roasted nuts, and use 1 tbsp of the corresponding nut oil in place of some of the extra-virgin olive oil.

∗ Use Asian-flavoured ingredients such as rice vinegar, light soy sauce, dashi and a little sesame oil to complement sashimi fish. Or assemble a dressing of ¼ cup lime juice, 1½ tbsp fish sauce, 1 seeded and finely chopped fresh small red chilli, 2 tsp caster sugar and 1 finely chopped small clove of garlic, stirring until sugar dissolves.

CLOCKWISE FROM FRONT: WATERCRESS, AVOCADO AND ORANGE SALAD;
ICEBERG WEDGES WITH BLUE CHEESE DRESSING; ITALIAN BITTER-LEAF SALAD

WATERCRESS, AVOCADO AND ORANGE SALAD

2 avocados

1 orange, peeled, segmented and chopped

2 cups watercress sprigs

¼ cup olive oil

1½ tbsp lime juice

1 Halve and seed avocados, then, using a spoon, scoop avocado flesh into a bowl and add orange and watercress.

2 Whisk together olive oil and lime juice and season to taste, then pour over salad and toss gently to combine.

Serves 4

ICEBERG WEDGES WITH BLUE CHEESE DRESSING

1 iceberg lettuce

BLUE CHEESE DRESSING

½ cup extra-virgin olive oil

2 tbsp red wine vinegar

1 tsp Dijon mustard

1 tsp caster sugar

1 tbsp pouring cream

150 gm full-flavoured blue cheese, crumbled

1 Remove outer leaves of lettuce and discard. Trim base of lettuce and cut lengthways into 6 wedges. Wash wedges, drain and pat dry.

2 For blue cheese dressing, process oil, vinegar, mustard, sugar and cream in a food processor until combined. Add cheese and pulse until smooth. Makes about 1 cup.

3 To serve, place lettuce wedges, cut-side up, on a plate and drizzle with blue cheese dressing.

Serves 6

ITALIAN BITTER-LEAF SALAD

Juice of 1 meyer lemon

¼ cup extra-virgin olive oil

1 bunch of rocket, trimmed

100 g wild rocket

1 radicchio, outer leaves discarded, leaves coarsely torn

1 witlof, leaves separated

1 small bulb of fennel, trimmed and shaved using a mandolin or vegetable peeler [see page 278]

This simple Italian country-style salad also works well with 1 tbsp aged balsamic vinegar instead of lemon juice.

1 Place lemon juice and olive oil in a small bowl, season to taste and whisk to combine.

2 Place remaining ingredients in a bowl, add dressing and toss to combine well, then serve immediately.

Serves 6

BABY HERB SALAD WITH ELDERFLOWER VINAIGRETTE

1 punnet each of baby coriander, baby red chard, baby lamb's lettuce [mâche], baby flat-leaf parsley, baby watercress and baby mizuna greens

½ cup elderflower sprigs [see Glossary]

2 tsp Dijon mustard

2 tsp honey

½ cup extra-virgin olive oil

ELDERFLOWER VINEGAR

2 cups red wine vinegar

¼ cup elderflower tea [see Glossary]

1 For elderflower vinegar, place ½ cup vinegar in a saucepan and bring to the boil over medium heat. Add elderflower tea and stir to combine, then remove from heat and leave for 10 minutes. Add elderflower mixture to remaining vinegar in a bowl and stir to combine. Transfer to a sterilised airtight container and refrigerate for 1 week before using. Elderflower vinegar will keep for up to 3 months. Makes about 2¼ cups.
2 Using kitchen scissors, snip baby herbs and leaves into a large bowl. Add elderflowers and gently stir to combine.
3 To make the vinaigrette, place 2 tbsp elderflower vinegar, mustard, honey and olive oil in a bowl, season to taste and whisk to combine.
4 Add elderflower vinaigrette to salad, toss gently to combine and serve immediately.
Serves 4

BUTTER LETTUCE, RADISH AND MINT SALAD

2 tbsp extra-virgin olive oil

3 tsp Champagne vinegar

½ tsp wholegrain mustard

1 small shallot, finely chopped

1 small butter lettuce, trimmed, outer leaves discarded, washed and torn into bite-size pieces

2 radishes, thinly sliced

⅓ cup mint leaves, torn

1 Whisk together oil, vinegar, mustard and shallot until well combined, then season to taste.
2 Place lettuce, radish and mint in a large bowl. Just before serving, add dressing and toss gently to combine.
Serves 4

BABY HERB SALAD WITH ELDERFLOWER VINAIGRETTE

classics

Certain salads are so right, such a happy balance of textures and flavours, that they live on from generation to generation. Some of these beloved classics were the inspiration of gifted chefs. The Caesar salad has been credited to both Giacomo Junia, an Italian chef in Chicago, and Caesar Cardini at his restaurant in Tijuana, Mexico, while the Waldorf salad was invented for the opening of New York's Waldorf Astoria hotel. Russian salad has been a star of the hors d'oeuvre course in grand hotels and restaurants for years.

Other salad classics are traditional 'folk' recipes that developed in a particular region as an especially good way to use the local produce. Greek horiatiki salad uses that country's abundant wild herbs, olives and feta cheese. Ratatouille salad is simply the cold version of the splendid French stew of Mediterranean vegetables. Italian panzanella originally included yesterday's leftover bread to make the dish filling enough for hungry peasants.

Most of the salads in this chapter are meant to stand alone as first courses or lunch dishes. Others are designed as magnificent accompaniments to plainly cooked meat, poultry or fish, and we've given ideas, in the recipes, for using them this way.

COLESLAW

¼ savoy cabbage [about 600g],
finely shredded

2 carrots, coarsely grated

2 stalks of celery, finely chopped

4 green onions, finely chopped

¼ cup finely chopped flat-leaf parsley

1 cup classic mayonnaise, with a little
water added if too thick [see page 19]

1 Combine all ingredients in a large bowl and mix well. Cover and refrigerate until ready to serve.

Serves 8 as an accompaniment

RADICCHIO SLAW WITH WALNUT OIL

1 Spanish onion, halved and thinly sliced

2 radicchio

2 bulbs of baby fennel [about 270g each],
halved and thinly sliced,
reserving green fronds

100 ml walnut oil

1½ tbsp chardonnay vinegar or
other aged white wine vinegar

60 g walnuts, roasted and coarsely chopped

1 Toss onion with 1 tsp sea salt and stand for 20 minutes, then rinse and drain well.
2 Trim the bases of the radicchio, discard dark outer leaves and shred finely. Wash radicchio, then spin dry in a salad spinner and place in a bowl with onion and fennel.
3 Whisk together walnut oil and vinegar in a small bowl and season to taste. Pour over salad, add walnuts and 2 tbsp chopped reserved fennel fronds and toss well to combine. Salad can be prepared 4 hours in advance.

Serves 8 as an accompaniment

WARM POTATO SALAD

100 g thinly sliced coppa or rindless bacon

1.25 kg nicola potatoes, scrubbed

½ cup sour cream

2 tbsp wholegrain mustard

1 tbsp honey

75 g cornichons, finely chopped [see Glossary]

1 small shallot, finely chopped

2 tbsp red wine vinegar

⅓ cup olive oil

1 bunch of chives, finely chopped

1 Place coppa on an oven tray and cook under a hot grill until browned. Cool, then tear coarsely.
2 Cook potatoes in a large saucepan of boiling salted water until tender, then drain. Cool slightly, then peel skins from potatoes and cut into 3-4mm thick slices.
3 Combine remaining ingredients in a large bowl, season to taste and mix well. Add potato slices and coppa and toss gently to coat.
Serves 6 as an accompaniment

CLOCKWISE FROM FRONT: RADICCHIO SLAW WITH WALNUT OIL; COLESLAW; WARM POTATO SALAD

CAPONATA

CAPONATA

1 kg eggplant, cut into 6cm pieces
Olive oil
1 onion, thinly sliced
5 stalks of celery, cut into 2cm pieces
200 g green olives, pitted and halved
2 tbsp drained capers
1½ cups passata [see Glossary]
2 tsp caster sugar
⅓ cup red wine vinegar
2 tsp Dutch-process cocoa [see Glossary]
70 g [½ cup] slivered almonds, roasted
Crispbread, to serve

1 Place eggplant in a colander, sprinkle with 1 tbsp sea salt and stand for 30 minutes. Rinse under cold running water and pat dry with absorbent paper.
2 Heat 2 tbsp olive oil in a large saucepan, add half the eggplant and cook until golden. Drain on absorbent paper. Repeat with more oil and remaining eggplant, then set aside.
3 Heat 2 tbsp oil in same pan and cook onion over low-medium heat for 5 minutes, then add celery and cook for another 2 minutes. Add olives, capers, passata, sugar and vinegar and simmer over medium heat for 10 minutes. Add eggplant and cocoa and stir occasionally over low-medium heat for another 15 minutes. Season to taste, remove from heat and cool. Cover and refrigerate overnight.
4 Bring caponata to room temperature 1 hour before serving, sprinkle with roasted almonds and serve with crispbread, cold meats and cheese, or as part of an antipasti selection.
Serves 6-8 as an accompaniment

PANZANELLA

1 red and 1 yellow capsicum
6 egg tomatoes, peeled,
    seeded and sliced lengthways
60 g [⅓ cup] small black olives, pitted
1 clove of garlic, finely chopped
1 shallot, finely chopped
½ cup extra-virgin olive oil
2 tbsp red wine vinegar
160 g day-old ciabatta, crust
    removed and cut into 2cm pieces
1 cup [loosely packed] basil leaves

1 Place capsicum on an oven tray and roast at 200C for 30 minutes or until skin blisters and blackens. Remove from oven, cover with foil and stand for 15 minutes. Peel skins, remove seeds and cut into 1cm slices lengthways, reserving juices. Cool.
2 Combine capsicum and their juices, tomatoes, olives, garlic, shallot, oil and vinegar and toss to combine. Stand for 30 minutes for flavours to develop. Just before serving, add bread and basil and toss to combine.
Serves 4 as a starter or light meal

CAPPON MAGRO

375 ml dry vermouth or dry white wine

2 shallots, thinly sliced

1 fresh bay leaf

¼ tsp each black peppercorns and fennel seeds

16 green scampi, heads discarded, cleaned

1 kg green king prawns, peeled and cleaned, leaving tails intact

3 ocean trout steaks [about 280g each], skinned and pin-boned [see Glossary]

600 g cleaned baby squid, scored and cut into 8mm-thick slices, tentacles reserved

800 g black mussels, scrubbed and bearded

Steamed asparagus, broccolini, zucchini flowers, quartered baby fennel and char-grilled ciabatta to serve

CAPPON MAGRO SAUCE

¾ cup [firmly packed] flat-leaf parsley, plunged into boiling water, refreshed in iced water and patted dry with absorbent paper

2 cloves of garlic, crushed

2 tbsp salted baby capers, rinsed and drained [see page 169]

2 anchovy fillets, coarsely chopped

1 tbsp pinenuts, lightly roasted

2 hard-boiled egg yolks

35 g [⅓ cup] fresh ciabatta crumbs, soaked in water and squeezed of excess liquid

⅔ cup extra-virgin olive oil

1 tbsp aged cabernet vinegar

12 Sicilian green olives, pitted and finely chopped [see Glossary]

2 tbsp finely chopped fennel

1 For cappon magro sauce, process parsley, garlic, capers, anchovies and pinenuts in a food processor until a coarse paste forms. Add egg yolks, soaked breadcrumbs, oil and vinegar and process until just combined. Transfer to a bowl, add remaining ingredients, season to taste and stir to combine. Cover closely with plastic wrap and refrigerate until needed. Makes about 2 cups. Sauce will keep, refrigerated in an airtight container, for up to 3 days.

2 Place vermouth, shallots, bay leaf, peppercorns and fennel seeds in a deep frying pan, cover with a lid and bring to the boil over high heat. Removing each batch with a slotted spoon before adding the next, add scampi and prawns and cook, covered, for 3-4 minutes, add ocean trout and cook, covered, for 2-3 minutes, add squid and cook, covered, for 1 minute, then add mussels and cook, covered, for 1-2 minutes or until shells just open.

3 Place poached seafood and steamed vegetables on a large plate and serve with cappon magro sauce and char-grilled ciabatta passed separately.

Serves 6 as a main course or 8 as a light meal

TUNA AND ARTICHOKE SALAD NICOISE

350 g baby green beans, trimmed

3 300g tuna steaks
  [about 2.5cm thick], halved

  Olive oil

250 g truss cherry tomatoes, separated

1 butter lettuce, trimmed, leaves
  separated, washed and dried

150 g preserved artichoke hearts
  in olive oil, drained, quartered

1 tbsp small capers

60 g small black olives

3 hard-boiled eggs, quartered

3 anchovy fillets, halved lengthways

NICOISE DRESSING

100 ml olive oil

½ clove of garlic

¼ cup [firmly packed] basil leaves

1½ tbsp aged white wine vinegar

1 For Niçoise dressing, process oil, garlic and basil in a small food processor until very finely chopped, then, just before serving, whisk in vinegar and season to taste. Makes about ¾ cup.
2 Cook beans in boiling salted water until almost tender, drain, refresh in iced water, then drain again.
3 Brush tuna steaks lightly on both sides with olive oil. Heat a heavy-based char-grill or frying pan until very hot and cook tuna, in batches, for 1½ minutes on each side for medium rare or until cooked to your liking. Remove tuna from pan and cool slightly. Add tomatoes to same pan, cover with a lid and, shaking pan occasionally, cook for 2-3 minutes or until tomatoes are just soft and the skins have burst.
4 Toss beans with 2 tbsp dressing. Place lettuce leaves over the base of 6 shallow bowls, then top with beans, tomatoes, artichokes, capers, olives and egg quarters. Place tuna pieces over salad with anchovies, drizzle with remaining dressing and serve immediately.
Serves 6 as a light meal

TUNISIAN-STYLE NICOISE SALAD

✱ Barbecue or char-grill 250g whole cherry tomatoes, turning over high heat until skins just burst. Roast, peel and thinly slice 2 yellow and 2 red capsicum, then place in a large bowl with cherry tomatoes, 185g can drained and flaked Italian-style tuna and ½ cup pitted kalamata olives. Combine ¼ cup extra-virgin olive oil, the juice of 1 lemon and ¼ tsp each of ground caraway and ground coriander, pour over salad, season to taste and toss to combine. Serve topped with 3 halved medium-boiled eggs and flatbread passed separately.
Serves 4

41

ESCALIVADA

2 red capsicum

2 large eggplant [about 1.2kg]

6 spring onions, trimmed
and halved lengthways

Extra-virgin olive oil

1 large clove of garlic, chopped

1 tbsp sherry vinegar [see page 15]

2 tbsp coarsely chopped flat-leaf parsley

2 tsp small capers in vinegar, drained

Crusty bread, to serve

Escalivada comes from the Catalan word escalivar, which means 'to char', because the vegetables were traditionally cooked over embers. Char-grilling or barbecuing are the ideal methods, as oven-roasting the vegetables does not achieve the smoky flavour that is the essence of the dish.

1 Char-grill or barbecue capsicum and eggplant on all sides until soft and tender, then transfer to a bowl, cover with plastic wrap and stand for 15 minutes. Peel capsicum and eggplant, then remove seeds from capsicum and tear into large pieces. Remove stem end of eggplant and tear eggplant lengthways into 6 pieces.
2 Lightly brush spring onions with olive oil, then char-grill or barbecue for 3-4 minutes on each side or until just tender and golden. Place char-grilled vegetables on a large platter or in separate bowls.
3 Place garlic and 1 tsp sea salt into a mortar and, using a pestle, pound until a smooth paste forms, then add ¼ cup olive oil, vinegar, parsley and capers. Season to taste with freshly ground black pepper, combine well and drizzle mixture over grilled vegetables. Serve warm or at room temperature with crusty or toasted bread, or as an accompaniment to roasted meat or fish.
Serves 6 as a starter or accompaniment

PESTLE AND MORTAR
While often associated with Asian cuisines, the use of a mortar and pestle is integral to a vast range of Spanish salad dressings and sauces, as well as the numerous egg-based aïoli and nut-based sauces, the most famous of which is romesco. Traditionally in Spain a wooden mortar and pestle is used to crush ingredients in order to remove essential oils, release their flavours and pound them so that they incorporate to form a paste-like consistency. This method is preferred to using a food processor which achieves a different result; finely chopping or blending ingredients, rather than crushing them, is not as effective in releasing flavours.

CAESAR SALAD

2 cos lettuce

½ day-old baguette or
4 thick slices of stale white bread

1 clove of garlic, halved

Olive oil, for shallow-frying

8 anchovy fillets, rinsed and dried

4 slices of prosciutto [optional],
grilled until crisp and broken into pieces

25 g [⅓ cup] shaved parmesan

CAESAR DRESSING

1 egg

2 cloves of garlic, crushed

2 anchovy fillets, rinsed, dried and mashed

1 tsp Worcestershire sauce

1 tbsp lemon juice

½ cup olive oil

20 g [¼ cup] grated parmesan

1 Discard large outer leaves of lettuces. Wash remaining leaves and dry thoroughly.

2 Remove crusts from bread, cut into 1.5cm-thick slices and rub both sides with garlic. Cut into 1.5cm cubes, then shallow-fry in hot olive oil until crisp and golden, or place on an oven tray, brush with olive oil and bake at 180C for 10 minutes or until crisp. Drain on absorbent paper.

3 For Caesar dressing, combine egg, garlic, anchovies, Worcestershire sauce and lemon juice in a food processor. With motor running, gradually add olive oil in a thin, steady stream until thick and creamy. Stir in parmesan and season to taste. Makes about 1 cup.

4 Place dressing in a serving bowl, add the cos leaves and roll gently to coat well. Serve topped with croutons, anchovy fillets, prosciutto [if using] and shaved parmesan.

Serves 4 as a starter or light meal

VARIATIONS

* Adding seafood, such as 1kg peeled, cooked king prawns with tails intact, or sliced medallions of cooked bug or lobster meat, provides a modern take on this faithful classic. In place of the traditional cos, either add 1 head of trimmed radicchio, with outer leaves discarded and inner leaves cut into bite-size pieces, or serve spoonfuls of salad in separated and trimmed radicchio leaves.

* The flavours of this anchovy-spiked dressing also work well with a warm potato salad. Cook 1kg scrubbed kipfler or nicola potatoes in boiling salted water until tender, cool slightly and cut into large pieces. Add torn pancetta and finely chopped chives, season to taste and stir to combine, then serve with char-grilled swordfish skewers. Alternatively, use the dressing as a dipping sauce for barbecued or char-grilled seafood.

* For Caesar sandwiches, rub 4 halved panini with a clove of garlic, brush with olive oil, then char-grill until lightly toasted. Spread half of each panini with Caesar dressing, then top with shredded cos, crisp grilled prosciutto and shaved Parmigiano Reggiano, top with remaining panini halves and serve immediately. Small versions can also be made using mini sourdough or ciabatta rolls and served as finger food or picnic fare.

GOAT'S CHEESE, PEAR AND HAZELNUT SALAD WITH BITTER LEAVES

300 g piece of streaky bacon,
rind removed, cut into 2cm pieces

2 tbsp extra-virgin olive oil

4 slices of sourdough bread,
crust removed, cut into 1cm pieces

45 g [⅓ cup] hazelnuts, roasted,
peeled and coarsely crushed

70 g watercress sprigs [about ⅓ bunch]

2 corella pears, cored and quartered

1 tbsp verjuice [see page 144]

1 shallot, finely chopped

2 150g logs of mature goat's cheese,
each cut widthways into 6 slices

1 Cook bacon in a heavy-based frying pan over low-medium heat until crisp and golden, then remove with a slotted spoon and drain on absorbent paper, reserving remaining fat in pan.
2 Add 1 tbsp olive oil to same pan and, when hot, add bread, toss to combine well and stir over low heat for 8-10 minutes or until crisp, then drain on absorbent paper.
3 Place bacon, croutons, hazelnuts, watercress and pears in a bowl.
4 Combine verjuice, shallot and remaining olive oil in a small bowl, season to taste, then pour over salad, toss to combine well and divide among 4 plates.
5 Place goat's cheese rounds on a baking paper-lined oven tray and cook under a hot grill for 2 minutes or until just melted and golden. Using a small spatula, divide grilled cheese among salads and serve immediately.
Serves 4 as a starter or light meal

RATATOUILLE

2 large eggplant [about 900g],
cut into 3cm pieces

⅓ cup olive oil

2 onions, thinly sliced

2 red capsicum, seeded
and cut into 3cm pieces

2 cloves of garlic, finely chopped

2 zucchini [about 800g], cut into 3cm pieces

3 large tomatoes, peeled,
seeded and cut into 3cm pieces

2 sprigs of fresh thyme

⅓ cup coarsely chopped
basil or flat-leaf parsley

1 Place eggplant in a colander over a bowl, sprinkle with salt and leave for 45 minutes, then rinse under running water and pat dry with absorbent paper.
2 Heat oil in a large heavy-based non-stick frying pan over medium heat. Add onion and cook for 10 minutes until soft and light golden. Add capsicum, eggplant and garlic and reduce heat to medium-low. Cover pan and cook for 30 minutes. Add zucchini, tomatoes and thyme, cover and cook for another 20 minutes. Season to taste and stir in basil or parsley. Serve hot or at room temperature. Ratatouille will keep, covered in the refrigerator, for up to 3 days.
Serves 6 as an accompaniment

HORIATIKI SALAD WITH PRAWNS AND HERB DRESSING

4 cups purslane, watercress sprigs or rocket

2 Lebanese cucumbers,
cut into 5mm-thick rounds

5 vine-ripened tomatoes,
halved and each cut into 8 wedges

1 white onion, peeled and thinly sliced

24 kalamata olives

150 g Greek feta, sliced

12 medium cooked prawns, peeled
and cleaned, leaving tails intact

Sprigs of Greek basil, to serve

HERB DRESSING

½ cup olive oil

¼ cup red wine vinegar

1 tbsp each mixed torn herbs, including
chervil, oregano, dill, mint and Greek basil

1 For herb dressing, combine all ingredients in a bowl and season to taste. Makes about ¾ cup.

2 Place purslane, cucumbers, tomatoes, onion, olives and feta in layers in 4 bowls, top each with 3 prawns and small sprigs of Greek basil and serve immediately, with herb dressing passed separately.

Serves 4 as a light meal

GREEK FETA

Feta, meaning 'slice', is a classic Greek cheese. Traditionally it is made from sheep's or goat's milk, though commercial producers now often make it with cow's milk. The milk is curdled with rennet and drained in a special mould or a cloth bag. It is then cut into large slices which are salted and packed in barrels filled with whey or brine for a week to several months.

GREEK BASIL

The basil used in this colourful traditional Greek country salad is prized for its anise-clove flavour. One of 150 species of basil, Greek basil features a robust flavour and small leaves, ideal for use in salads or as a garnish, especially for dishes that incorporate tomatoes. With its compact shape, the herb grows well in small pots on windowsills.

WALDORF SALAD WITH CHICKEN

2 skinless chicken breast fillets

1 fresh or dried bay leaf

3 black peppercorns

2 red apples, quartered, cored, thinly sliced and tossed in 2 tbsp lemon juice

3 stalks of celery, string removed with a vegetable peeler, cut into 3mm-thick slices

¼ cup chopped celery leaves [from heart of celery]

50 g [½ cup] coarsely chopped walnuts

½ cup classic mayonnaise [see page 19]

18 baby cos leaves, to serve

1 Place chicken, bay leaf and peppercorns in a saucepan and add just enough water to cover. Bring to the boil, reduce heat, then simmer chicken over very low heat for 15-20 minutes or until just cooked through. Remove from heat and cool in poaching liquid.

2 Finely shred chicken and combine with apples, celery, celery leaves and half the walnuts in a bowl. Add mayonnaise, season to taste, then stir to combine well.

3 To serve, spoon salad into lettuce cups and scatter with the remaining walnuts.

Serves 6 as a starter or light meal

VARIATIONS

* For a twist on the classic Waldorf salad, use hot-smoked trout, pear and pecans in place of chicken, apple and walnuts. Place flaked flesh of a skinned and pin-boned hot-smoked trout, 2 quartered, cored and thinly sliced beurre bosc pears tossed in 2 tbsp lemon juice, ½ cup coarsely chopped roasted pecans, and ½ cup each crème fraîche and mayonnaise in a bowl, season to taste and stir to combine, then serve in trimmed witlof leaves.

* For a Waldorf-inspired coleslaw, substitute chicken with ½ small finely shredded red cabbage. Place ⅓ cup each mayonnaise and sour cream, 1 tbsp Dijon mustard and 2 tsp red wine vinegar in a bowl, season to taste and whisk to combine, then add to salad and stir gently to combine. Top with crumbled blue cheese, if desired. Serve as an accompaniment to grilled chicken or as part of a banquet selection.

* To transform this salad into a more substantial meal, add 250g halved globe grapes, ¼ cup dried sour cherries and shredded smoked duck breast or poached turkey breast, instead of chicken. For a more tangy dressing, place ½ cup each mayonnaise and Greek-style yoghurt, ½ tsp each ground allspice and cumin and a pinch of cayenne in a bowl, season to taste and whisk to combine, then add to salad.

LOBSTER RUSSIAN SALAD WITH VODKA MAYONNAISE

LOBSTER RUSSIAN SALAD WITH VODKA MAYONNAISE

1 kg kipfler potatoes, scrubbed
100 g baby green beans, trimmed
100 g baby butter beans, trimmed
100 g sugar snap peas, trimmed
2 cooked lobsters [about 700g each], peeled, cleaned and cut into 1.5cm-thick slices

VODKA MAYONNAISE

1 clove of garlic, coarsely chopped
2 egg yolks
2 tsp Dijon mustard
1¼ cups sunflower oil
2 tsp vodka, or to taste

1 For vodka mayonnaise, place garlic on a chopping board, sprinkle with a large pinch of sea salt and, using the flat side of a large knife, crush garlic and salt together until a smooth paste forms. Place egg yolks, garlic paste and mustard in a bowl and stir to combine. Whisking continuously, gradually add oil, drop by drop at first, then in a thin, steady stream until thick and emulsified. Add vodka and whisk until incorporated, then season to taste with sea salt, cover closely with plastic wrap and refrigerate until needed. Makes about 1¼ cups.
2 Cook potatoes in boiling salted water until tender, then drain, cool slightly, cut each lengthways into thirds and set aside.
3 Blanch green beans, butter beans and sugar snap peas separately in boiling salted water for 2 minutes or until just tender, then drain, refresh in iced water and drain again.
4 Place potatoes, beans, sugar snap peas and lobster in a large bowl, then add ⅓ cup vodka mayonnaise, thinned with 1 tbsp warm water, if necessary. Season to taste and stir gently to combine. Divide salad among bowls and serve immediately, with remaining vodka mayonnaise passed separately.
Serves 4 as a light meal

PRAWN COCKTAIL

1 kg cooked tiger prawns
3 iceberg lettuce leaves, finely shredded
1 firm ripe avocado, peeled, seeded and diced

COCKTAIL SAUCE

1 cup classic mayonnaise [see page 19]
2 tbsp tomato ketchup
1 tsp Worcestershire sauce
1 tsp brandy
Tabasco sauce, to taste
1-2 tsp lemon juice
Lemon wedges and buttered slices of brown bread, to serve

1 For cocktail sauce, place mayonnaise, tomato ketchup, Worcestershire sauce and brandy in a small bowl, season to taste and combine well, then add Tabasco and lemon juice to taste. Cover closely with plastic wrap and refrigerate until needed. Makes about 1⅓ cups.
2 Reserve 6 prawns in their shells and peel and clean the remainder.
3 Divide lettuce among 6 stemmed glasses or glass bowls. Top with avocado, then peeled prawns. Spoon cocktail sauce over, garnish with reserved prawns and a wedge of lemon and serve with slices of buttered brown bread.
Serves 6 as a starter

salads to go

Salads to take on a picnic should follow the rules that apply to all picnic food. They should be easy to transport, ready to serve without effort or mess, not fussy about the temperature at which they're eaten, and able to be held in the hand or comfortably managed with only a fork.

One excellent idea is to combine the salad part of the meal with the bread part, so that each person gets a serving of salad neatly enclosed in a roll, pita or tortilla, a thick slice of baguette or a chunk of Italian bread. Salads to be served in bowls, such as the BLT salad on page 64, work well, too. Consider a combination picnic – make a finger-food salad, such as the delicious eggplant and tuna rolls on page 68, purchase a prepared item such as dolmades, and add raw fresh vegetables. Chunks or batons of cucumber, carrot, celery, spring onion, capsicum and zucchini work well, as does a handful of cherry tomatoes, radishes [whole or halved, depending on size] and perhaps baby squash or button mushrooms, with aïoli, mayonnaise or yoghurt for dipping. Be sure to supply plenty of paper napkins.

BEEF TAQUITOS WITH CORN AND BLACK BEAN SALSA

½ cup olive oil

1 clove of garlic, crushed

½ tsp ground white pepper

½ tsp ground black pepper

½ tsp ground cumin

500 g minced beef

⅓ cup oregano leaves, chopped, plus extra, to serve

8 15cm corn tortillas

200 g mozzarella, grated

CORN AND BLACK BEAN SALSA

1 corn cob, husks and silks removed

1 dried ancho chilli [see Glossary]

2½ tbsp olive oil

40g butter

1 small onion, chopped

¾ cup canned black beans, or ½ cup dried beans, soaked in cold water overnight, cooked in boiling water for about 30 minutes or until tender, then drained well

¼ cup oregano, chopped

1 For corn and black bean salsa, cook corn in boiling salted water for 5 minutes, then drain. When cool enough to handle, remove kernels [see page 253].

2 Using tongs, hold ancho chilli over a gas flame or heat gently under a grill until chilli begins to expand and soften; do not let it blacken, as it will become bitter and hard. Cool, then remove seeds and veins, rinse under hot water and cut into thin strips.

3 Heat olive oil and butter in a frying pan, add onion and chilli and cook over low heat for 3-4 minutes, then add corn kernels and black beans and cook for another 5 minutes. Cool to room temperature, then stir in oregano.

4 Heat ¼ cup olive oil in a frying pan, add garlic, peppers, cumin, beef and ¼ tsp salt and cook over medium-high heat for 5 minutes or until beef is browned. Stir in oregano, then cool to room temperature.

5 To make taquitos, cut tortillas in half and place a spoonful of beef mixture at one end of each half, top with a little cheese, then roll up tightly into a small cigar shape and secure with a toothpick.

6 Heat remaining oil in a frying pan and cook taquitos, turning frequently, for 3-4 minutes, over medium heat until golden all over. Remove toothpicks. Divide corn and black bean salsa among 4 warm plates, place taquitos on top and sprinkle with extra oregano.

Serves 4

VARIATIONS

* This beef mixture makes a delicious filling for empanadas, also ideal picnic fare. Add chopped hard-boiled eggs, coarsely chopped flat-leaf parsley and raisins to beef mixture. Cut 8cm rounds from prepared puff pastry sheets, place tablespoonfuls of beef mixture in the centre of pastry rounds, fold over to enclose filling, forming a half-moon shape, then crimp edges to seal. Bake empanadas at 180C until golden, then serve warm or at room temperature.

* For pork picadillo-filled taquitos, heat a little vegetable oil in a frying pan, add coarsely chopped onion, crushed garlic, finely chopped red jalapeño chillies and minced pork, then cook over high heat until meat browns. Add ½ tsp each allspice, cinnamon and ground cumin, a can of chopped egg tomatoes, roasted almond slivers and currants and cook until mixture thickens. Add lime juice to taste, then use pork picadillo instead of beef mixture to fill taquitos.

STUFFED PEPPERS

6-8 baby red capsicum, preferably
Bella Rosso peppers [see page 200]

¼ cup extra-virgin olive oil

100g crusty Italian bread, crusts
removed, cut into large pieces

45 g [¼ cup] baby salted capers,
rinsed and drained [see page 169]

60 g [½ cup] Ligurian olives
or other small black olives,
pitted and halved [see page 241]

6 anchovy fillets, coarsely chopped

1 clove of garlic, finely chopped

¼ cup flat-leaf parsley leaves,
coarsely chopped

¼ cup basil leaves, coarsely chopped

1 tbsp small flat-leaf parsley leaves,
to serve, optional

1 Rub capsicum with ¼ tsp olive oil, place on an oven tray and roast at 250C for 10-12 minutes or until skins blister. Transfer to a bowl, cover with plastic wrap and cool.
2 Process bread in a food processor for 1-2 minutes until coarse breadcrumbs form. Heat 2 tbsp oil in a heavy-based frying pan, add breadcrumbs and stir over medium heat for 3-5 minutes or until golden and crisp.
3 Carefully peel capsicum and remove cores and seeds, keeping their shape intact.
4 Combine remaining ingredients, except parsley leaves, in a bowl and stir in the breadcrumbs. Fill capsicum with breadcrumb mixture, drizzle with remaining oil and serve scattered with parsley if using.
Serves 4-6

PEPPERED MUSSELS

500 g small black mussels, bearded

Rind of 1 lemon

¼ cup lemon juice

1 tsp black peppercorns,
coarsely crushed

¼ cup flat-leaf parsley,
coarsely chopped

Though it is important to beard the mussels, do not wash them, as this will affect the flavour of the dish.

1 Place mussels in a large frying pan with 1 tbsp water, then cover and cook for 1 minute or until mussels open, discarding unopened mussels. Add lemon rind, juice and peppercorns and cook for another 30 seconds, then remove from heat, stir through parsley and serve.
Serves 4-6

DROWNED OCTOPUS

500 g baby octopus

2½ tbsp extra-virgin olive oil

6-8 large cherry tomatoes, quartered

1 small red chilli, seeded and finely sliced

1 clove of garlic, finely chopped

2 tbsp oregano leaves

1 Bring 1 litre salted water to the boil. Add octopus and bring back to the boil, then drain and discard cooking liquid. Remove and discard heads and beaks, then cut tentacles into quarters.
2 Heat 2 tbsp olive oil in a large heavy-based frying pan, add octopus and cook over high heat for 30 seconds. Add remaining ingredients and cook for another 30 seconds. Remove from heat, season to taste and serve drizzled with remaining olive oil.
Serves 4-6

To me a salad is an appetiser. Something to arouse my tastebuds in anticipation of a great meal to come. It can also act as a snack when you don't want to eat something heavy, like late at night when you're watching a film. My favourite salad of all time is simply goat's cheese, cherry tomatoes and avocado drizzled with good olive oil, sea salt and maybe some balsamic vinegar.

Con Nemitsas

SHEFTALIA WITH PITA BREAD, SALAD AND YOGHURT

Con Nemitsas – Demcos Seafood, Sydney

500	g minced beef
500	g minced pork
2	large onions, coarsely chopped
	Grated rind of 1 lemon
1	tsp ground cinnamon
¼	cup flat-leaf parsley, coarsely chopped
750	g pork caul fat, rinsed well, then soaked in salted water for 10 minutes and drained [see Glossary]
	Small oval pita bread pockets
	Coarsely chopped egg tomatoes, combined extra chopped flat-leaf parsley and onion, and Greek-style yoghurt, to serve

1 Combine beef and pork mince, onions, lemon rind, cinnamon and flat-leaf parsley in a bowl and mix well, then season to taste. Divide mixture into 16 [about ⅓ cup each] and shape into 10cm logs.
2 Cut off a piece of caul fat 20-25cm long, place a meat log at one end and roll over once, then fold in sides and continue to roll several times until mince is enclosed well, trimming any excess caul fat. Repeat with remaining caul fat and mince.
3 Barbecue sheftalia, in batches, on a barbecue flat plate, turning frequently, over medium heat for 10-15 minutes or until cooked through. Barbecue pita pockets for 15-20 seconds on each side or until warmed through, then cut in half and fill each half with a couple of sheftalia, tomatoes and combined chopped flat-leaf parsley and onion. Serve immediately with Greek-style yoghurt to the side.
Serves 8

MARINATED PIRI PIRI CHICKEN WITH CUCUMBER SALAD AND LEBANESE BREAD

2   cloves of garlic, crushed

6   fresh small red chillies, coarsely chopped

⅓   cup lemon juice

1   cup olive oil

¼   cup white wine vinegar

2   tbsp chopped oregano

2   tsp sweet paprika

1.8 kg chicken thigh fillets [about 15]

    Lebanese bread, to serve

CUCUMBER SALAD

⅓   cup white wine vinegar

2   tsp caster sugar

3   Lebanese cucumbers, halved lengthways
    and thinly sliced on the diagonal

1   green capsicum, seeded and thinly sliced

2   egg tomatoes, chopped

1   tbsp coarsely chopped dill

1   tbsp coarsely chopped oregano

1 Process garlic, chillies, lemon juice and olive oil until well combined. Transfer to a large bowl, add vinegar, oregano, paprika and chicken and mix well. Cover and refrigerate for at least 8 hours or overnight.

2 For cucumber salad, combine vinegar and sugar, season to taste and mix well. Combine remaining ingredients, add vinegar mixture and toss gently to combine.

3 Char-grill or barbecue drained chicken, in batches, for 2-3 minutes on each side until cooked through. Slice and serve with salad wrapped in Lebanese bread.

Serves 8

CHILLI

Piri piri is the Swahili word for chilli and piri piri sauce is named after the piri piri chilli, traditionally the key ingredient in this spicy Portuguese sauce. Also known as pil pil chillies, piri piri are medium sized, bright red, very hot chillies preserved in brine and sold in jars. As they are not available in Australia, this recipe uses fresh small red chillies with the seeds intact instead. The seeds and pith of a chilli contain most of its capsaicin, the volatile oil that generates its heat, which is why including the seeds increases the heat level of a dish.

BLT SALAD

16 truss cherry tomatoes

3 sprigs of marjoram [see Glossary]

2 cloves of garlic, peeled

   Olive oil

½ baguette, cut into 1cm-thick slices

1 egg yolk

1 tsp Dijon mustard

12 rashers of streaky bacon

2 baby cos, outer leaves
   discarded, halved lengthways

1 Place tomatoes, marjoram, 1 clove of garlic and ½ cup olive oil in a shallow ovenproof dish, season to taste, then roast at 200C for 20 minutes or until tomatoes are just beginning to burst. Remove from oven and cool to room temperature. Strain tomatoes and garlic through a sieve and reserve liquid. Using the back of a knife, crush cooked garlic and ½ tsp sea salt on a work surface to make a smooth paste.

2 Brush bread slices on both sides liberally with oil, place on a heavy-based oven tray and bake at 180C for 20 minutes, turning once during cooking, or until golden on each side. Remove from oven and rub one side with remaining garlic clove, then coarsely break croutons into large pieces.

3 Combine egg yolk, mustard and garlic paste in a bowl, then, whisking continuously, gradually add ½ cup cooled reserved liquid, drop by drop, then in a thin, steady stream until mixture is thick and emulsified. Season to taste. Makes about ½ cup.

4 Cook bacon in a large heavy-based frying pan over medium heat until crisp on both sides, then drain on absorbent paper.

5 Divide lettuce among 4 plates. Top with tomatoes, bacon and croutons, drizzle with a little dressing, then serve immediately, with remaining dressing passed separately.

Serves 4

OCEAN TROUT MUFFULETTA

2 zucchini, thinly sliced lengthways

Olive oil

2 tbsp drained capers

1 cup [firmly packed] flat-leaf parsley

1 tbsp chopped dill

1 tbsp chopped chives

1 round Italian-style loaf [about 23cm]

600 g poached ocean trout fillets

4 hard-boiled eggs, peeled and sliced

75 g [1½ cups] rocket leaves, trimmed

Classic mayonnaise [see page 19] combined with grated lemon rind, to taste, to serve

1 Brush zucchini with a little olive oil, season to taste and grill under a hot grill until lightly browned.

2 Process capers, herbs and ⅓ cup olive oil until nearly smooth and season to taste.

3 Using a serrated knife, cut top from bread and reserve. Hollow out bread, leaving a 1cm-thick shell, then brush interior and underside of reserved lid with herb mixture. Layer half the zucchini, ocean trout, egg and rocket leaves inside loaf, repeat with remaining zucchini, ocean trout, egg and rocket, then replace lid. Wrap in plastic wrap and place on a tray, cover with another tray and weigh down with a brick or heavy cans of food. Refrigerate for 2 hours or overnight.

4 Serve muffuletta cut into wedges, with lemon mayonnaise.

Serves 8

BARBECUED CHICKEN, WATERMELON AND MINT SALAD

6 chicken thigh fillets [about 750g]

Juice of 2 limes, plus 1 tbsp extra

Olive oil

2 cloves of garlic

¼ tsp cayenne

⅓ cup mint leaves, plus ¼ cup extra, torn

3 cups chopped seedless yellow or red watermelon flesh

1 cos, leaves separated, washed and torn

1 tbsp white wine vinegar

Warm tortillas, to serve

1 Place chicken, lime juice and 1 tbsp olive oil in a glass or ceramic bowl and toss to coat chicken well.

2 Place garlic, 1 tsp sea salt, cayenne and mint leaves in a mortar and, using a pestle, grind to a paste, then rub over chicken. Cover and refrigerate for 20 minutes.

3 Barbecue or char-grill chicken for 4-5 minutes on each side or until tender, cool slightly, then shred coarsely and place in a bowl. Add watermelon, extra torn mint leaves and torn cos leaves, drizzle with ¼ cup olive oil, white wine vinegar and extra lime juice and toss gently to combine. Serve immediately with warm tortillas.

Serves 4

FIG, PROSCIUTTO, BAKED RICOTTA AND WILD ROCKET LOAF

1   rustic Italian ring-shaped loaf
    Extra-virgin olive oil
300 g baked ricotta, thinly sliced
150 g sliced prosciutto
5   ripe figs, sliced widthways
50 g wild rocket

1 Cut loaf in half widthways, scoop about 1.5cm bread from each half, then drizzle inside of loaf generously with olive oil.
2 Place ricotta slices over bread base, season to taste with freshly ground black pepper, then top with prosciutto, figs and rocket.
3 Replace top half of loaf, then, using kitchen string, tie loaf firmly at 5cm intervals. Wrap loaf firmly with plastic wrap, then refrigerate. Serve loaf cut into wedges.
Serves 6-8

GRILLED EGGPLANT WITH TUNA, BASIL AND CAPER STUFFING

2   eggplant [about 800g], cut lengthways into 7mm-thick slices
    Olive oil
220 g can tuna in oil, drained
⅔   cup fresh white breadcrumbs
2   tbsp small capers
2½ tbsp finely torn basil leaves
100 ml classic mayonnaise [see page 19]

1 Sprinkle eggplant slices with salt, layer in a colander and leave to drain for 30 minutes. Rinse slices, pat dry with absorbent paper, brush all over with olive oil, then char-grill or barbecue on each side for 2 minutes or until just tender. Cool.
2 Combine tuna, breadcrumbs, capers, basil leaves and mayonnaise and season to taste.
3 Place 1 tbsp tuna mixture along wide end of each eggplant slice and roll up to form rolls.
Makes about 18 rolls

FIG, PROSCIUTTO, BAKED RICOTTA AND WILD ROCKET LOAF

PAN BAGNAT

PAN BAGNAT

⅓ cup olive oil

2 Spanish onions, thinly sliced

1 red capsicum, seeded and thinly sliced

2 tbsp red wine vinegar

1 baguette or 6 bread rolls

1 clove of garlic, halved

1 cup [firmly packed] basil leaves

2 egg tomatoes, thinly sliced

80 g sopressa [see Glossary], thinly sliced, optional

¼ cup good-quality tapenade

1 Heat oil in a heavy-based frying pan, add onion and cook over medium heat for 10 minutes or until soft. Add capsicum and cook for another 10 minutes, then stir in vinegar until evaporated. Remove from heat and cool.

2 Cut baguette lengthways so that top crust or lid is approximately one-third of the thickness of the baguette and base is two-thirds. Scoop out some of the bread from base leaving a 1.5cm shell, then rub the garlic halves over cut sides of bread.

3 Spread the onion mixture evenly along the length of base, top with basil leaves, then layer with tomatoes and sopressa, if using. Spread tapenade over inside of lid and spoon over sopressa. Replace lid, then wrap baguette tightly in plastic wrap and refrigerate for at least 2 hours for flavours to develop. To serve, unwrap baguette and cut into 6 pieces.

Serves 6

SPINACH AND PARMESAN FRITTATA ROLLS WITH SEMI-DRIED TOMATOES

500 g spinach [1 bunch], trimmed and washed

6 eggs

125 g grated parmesan

1 tbsp olive oil

8 small bread rolls

100 g semi-dried tomatoes

1 Add spinach to a hot, lightly oiled frying pan and toss over high heat until wilted. Cool. Squeeze excess liquid from spinach and chop finely.

2 Whisk eggs, grated parmesan and spinach until well combined, then season to taste. Heat oil in a 26cm non-stick frying pan, add egg mixture and cook over low-medium heat until mixture is set around edges but still slightly runny in the middle. Cook under a hot grill until middle is set and top browned. Cool in pan, then cut into wedges.

3 Split bread rolls in half and fill with wedges of frittata and semi-dried tomatoes.

Serves 8

middle eastern & north african

Western taste is moving more and more towards the Middle Eastern approach to food, with its healthy emphasis on grains, nuts, pulses and vegetables, made irresistible with marvellous combinations of spices and herbs. Most of us have enjoyed the most famous Middle Eastern salad, tabbouleh, with its perfect balance of earthy burghul, refreshing herbs and the sharp tang of lemon. Like all the salads in this chapter, it is a wonderful party dish.

Some are complete in themselves as a summer lunch or a first or even main course. Others are perfect to team with grilled or roasted meat, chicken or fish, making them great choices for a barbecue. There are also recipes for the delightful institution of the mezze table, where a magnificent array of small appetisers, dips and snacks invites leisurely consumption.

Middle Eastern cooks adore colour and pattern, and great care is taken with the presentation of dishes, so think in terms of arranging your ingredients decoratively, or adding embellishments such as olives, tomato or cucumber slices, capsicum strips or fresh herbs.

middle eastern ingredients

POMEGRANATE MOLASSES [1]
A thick syrup made from boiled-down pomegranate juice. The name molasses refers to its consistency and colour, not its taste, which is sweet/sharp and slightly astringent.

**ROSEWATER [2],
ORANGE FLOWER WATER**
These gloriously fragrant flavourings for confectionery or desserts are distilled from fresh flowers selected for their intense scent. They are usually used in syrups to be poured over filo pastries.

COUSCOUS [3], MOGHRABIEH [5]
The staple cereal of North Africa, couscous consists of fine semolina [the first, grainy millings of the floury part of wheat grains, called the endosperm], combined with flour, salt and water to make tiny pellets. Traditionally, couscous is first moistened to allow the grains to swell, then steamed over the pot in which the meat and vegetables for the meal are simmering. It can also be bought pre-cooked.

Moghrabieh is couscous with larger grains, made from coarser semolina. It is sometimes called pearl couscous.

HARISSA [4]
A fiery Tunisian paste made by pounding chilli with garlic, spices and herbs. It is used for cooked meats such as kebabs and goes on the table as an all-purpose condiment. It is available in tubes, tins and jars at Middle Eastern grocers and some supermarkets and delicatessens.

TAHINI [6]
A soft paste made from ground sesame seeds, either toasted [which have more flavour] or untoasted. Best known as an ingredient in the chickpea-based dip, hummus.

ZA'ATAR [7]
A blend of ground dried thyme, sesame seeds, sumac and salt, available ready-mixed at Middle Eastern grocers, specialist spice shops and select grocers.

SUMAC [8]
A dark red spice made from the ground berries of the sumac tree, which grows in Turkey and other parts of the Mediterranean and Middle Eastern regions. Ground sumac has a refreshing, fruity sourness.

CORIANDER SEEDS [9]
Pale brown coriander seeds, the kind you will usually see, have a delicious lemon-with-a-touch-of-sage flavour. Less commonly, there is a yellow-green variety with a taste more reminiscent of the fresh herb.

PRESERVED LEMONS [10]
These are lemons preserved in salt and lemon juice. The flesh is removed before using, only the skin being eaten. The flavour of preserved lemons is strong, very different from fresh lemon.

DATES [11]
You can buy dates fresh or semi-dried. Fresh dates have smooth, glossy, golden-brown skin and a soft interior. Semi-dried are darker and wrinkled, with a firm, fudgy texture. They vary from handsome, well-separated specimens, often packed in boxes, to shapeless ones compressed into blocks. The shapely ones are good for stuffing, the shapeless ones are ideal for cooking.

BURGHUL
To make burghul, cracked wheat is hulled, parboiled so that it becomes lighter-textured and milder-flavoured, then dried. It needs no further cooking but, before use, is soaked for two hours in cold water to soften and swell the grains. Burghul is best known as an ingredient in the refreshing Lebanese salad tabbouleh.

RAS EL HANOUT
A traditional Moroccan mixture of up to 20 spices, varying from one spice merchant to another but always a subtle, spicy blend with a touch of heat.

CLOCKWISE FROM BOTTOM:
EGGPLANT WITH POMEGRANATE AND WALNUT DIP;
CUCUMBER AND YOGHURT SALAD;
MOROCCAN CARROT SALAD

EGGPLANT WITH POMEGRANATE AND WALNUT DIP

3 small eggplant, cut into 1cm-thick slices
¼ cup olive oil
2 tbsp white wine vinegar
2 tbsp coarsely chopped flat-leaf parsley
Pomegranate seeds, optional, to serve

POMEGRANATE AND WALNUT DIP

110 g walnuts, coarsely chopped
¼ round Lebanese bread
[about 20g], torn into small pieces
1½ tsp ground cumin
1 tsp chilli flakes
½ cup olive oil
2 tbsp pomegranate molasses [see Glossary]
1 tbsp tomato paste

1 For pomegranate and walnut dip, process walnuts, bread, spices, 1 tsp salt and ¼ cup water in a food processor until finely ground. Add remaining ingredients and process until well combined, then transfer to an airtight container and refrigerate for up to 2 weeks. Makes about 1¼ cups.

2 Sprinkle eggplant slices with salt, layer in a colander over a bowl and leave to drain for 30 minutes. Rinse eggplant and pat dry with absorbent paper. Toss eggplant in a bowl with olive oil, then barbecue or char-grill, in batches, over medium heat for 2 minutes on each side or until tender. Transfer to a large plate and layer in overlapping slices. Drizzle with vinegar, top with spoonfuls of pomegranate and walnut dip and serve scattered with parsley and pomegranate seeds, if using.

Serves 8 as an accompaniment or mezze

CUCUMBER AND YOGHURT SALAD

3 Lebanese cucumbers,
peeled, and finely chopped
1 clove of garlic, finely chopped
400 g Greek-style yoghurt
2 tsp coarsely chopped fresh mint
1½ tbsp extra-virgin olive oil

1 Place cucumber in a colander over a bowl, sprinkle with 1 tsp sea salt and stand for 1 hour, then drain well and pat dry with absorbent paper.

2 Combine cucumber, garlic, yoghurt and half the mint, then transfer to a small bowl. Serve drizzled with olive oil and scattered with remaining mint. Makes about 2½ cups.

Serves 8 as an accompaniment or mezze

MOROCCAN CARROT SALAD

3 bunches baby carrots,
peeled, tops trimmed
1 tbsp honey
Olive oil
1 tsp cumin seeds
1 tsp each sweet paprika
and ground cinnamon
2 tbsp lemon juice
2 tbsp each chopped coriander
and chopped flat-leaf parsley
60 g pinenuts, roasted

1 Combine carrots, honey, 2 tbsp olive oil and cumin seeds in a roasting pan, season to taste and toss well to combine. Roast at 190C for 20 minutes or until carrots are tender and lightly browned.

2 Dry-fry paprika and cinnamon in a small frying pan until fragrant, add 2 tbsp olive oil and lemon juice. Transfer carrot mixture to a platter, add spice mixture and herbs, season to taste and mix well. Serve warm or at room temperature, topped with pinenuts.

Serves 4-6 as an accompaniment or mezze

MOROCCAN SALAD WITH TAHINI DRESSING

1 bunch of rocket, trimmed
Sprigs of dill, mint and flat-leaf parsley
4 hard-boiled eggs, quartered
¼ red cabbage, finely shredded
1 large carrot, coarsely grated
6 radishes, coarsely grated
Lebanese bread, to serve

TAHINI DRESSING
1 clove of garlic
¼ cup tahini [see page 74]
Juice of 1 lemon

1 For tahini dressing, place garlic and a pinch of sea salt in a mortar and, using a pestle, pound to a paste. Transfer to a small bowl, add tahini and lemon juice and stir to combine. Add enough water to make a smooth dressing the consistency of double cream and season to taste. Makes about 1⅓ cups.
2 Combine rocket on a large plate with herbs and eggs, then arrange vegetables separately in a bowl. Drizzle with tahini dressing, or serve dressing passed separately, with Lebanese bread.
Serves 4 as an accompaniment or mezze

WHITE BEANS WITH TAHINI

400 g [2 cups] dried white beans [haricot or great northern], soaked in cold water overnight, then drained
¼ cup tahini [see page 74]
1 clove of garlic, finely chopped
⅓ cup lemon juice
2 tsp cumin seeds, dry-roasted
2 tbsp Middle Eastern verjuice or Australian verjuice [see page 144]
2 tsp sweet paprika
⅓ cup extra-virgin olive oil
2 tbsp chopped flat-leaf parsley
75 g pinenuts, roasted

1 Cook drained beans in plenty of boiling water for 50 minutes or until tender, then drain and keep warm.
2 Meanwhile, place tahini, garlic, lemon juice, cumin seeds and verjuice in a bowl, season to taste and whisk to combine well. Place beans in a large bowl and, while still warm, add tahini mixture and mix gently. Cover and stand at room temperature for 1 hour for flavours to develop.
3 Whisk paprika into olive oil in a small bowl and stand for 30 minutes or until paprika settles in base of bowl, then carefully spoon off oil. Stir parsley and three-quarters of the pinenuts into beans, then drizzle with paprika oil and scatter with remaining nuts.
Serves 8 as an accompaniment or mezze

WARM MOGHRABIEH SALAD WITH BARBECUED FISH BROCHETTES AND ALMOND TARATOR

165 g [1 cup] moghrabieh [see Glossary]
    Extra-virgin olive oil

800 g blue-eye trevalla or other firm-fleshed
    white fish, cut into 3-4cm pieces

  1 tbsp za'atar [see page 74]
    Grated rind and juice of
    1 large lemon, plus 1 lemon

 12 bamboo skewers, soaked
    in water for 20 minutes

100 g watercress or purslane, picked

125 g cherry or grape tomatoes, halved
    Lemon wedges, optional, to serve

ALMOND TARATOR

  1 large clove of garlic, finely chopped

 ½ tsp sea salt flakes

 80 g [½ cup] blanched whole almonds, roasted

 35 g [½ cup] fresh white breadcrumbs
    Juice of 1 lemon

 ¾ cup olive oil

1 For almond tarator, place garlic on a work surface, sprinkle with sea salt and, using the back of a large knife, crush garlic until a smooth paste forms. Transfer garlic paste to the bowl of a food processor, add almonds and breadcrumbs and process until finely chopped, then add lemon juice and 2 tbsp water and process to combine well. With motor running, add olive oil in a thin, steady stream until mixture is thick and emulsified, then transfer to a bowl and, using a wooden spoon, slowly stir in ⅓ cup water or enough to form a smooth, thick sauce. Season to taste, then cover closely with plastic wrap and refrigerate until needed. Makes about 2 cups.

2 Cook moghrabieh in a large saucepan of boiling water for 20-25 minutes or until tender, drain, transfer to a bowl, stir in 1 tbsp olive oil and 1 tsp sea salt, then set aside.

3 Meanwhile, place fish, za'atar, grated lemon rind and 2 tbsp olive oil in a bowl, season to taste and stir to coat. Cover with plastic wrap and leave for 10 minutes. Thread 3 pieces of fish on each soaked skewer, then char-grill or barbecue over high heat, turning halfway, for 4-5 minutes or until just cooked through.

4 Remove top and bottom from lemon, then cut into 8 wedges and remove seeds and core from each wedge. Thinly slice each wedge widthways into thin slivers. Add lemon slivers, lemon juice, ¼ cup olive oil, watercress and tomatoes to warm moghrabieh, season to taste and toss gently to combine.

5 Divide warm moghrabieh salad among shallow bowls, top each with 2 fish skewers, then serve immediately with lemon wedges to the side and tarator passed separately.

Serves 6

LAMB, CHICKPEA AND SUMAC SALAD

¾ cup extra-virgin olive oil

¼ cup sumac [see page 74]

1 tsp sweet paprika

600 g lamb fillets, trimmed

250 g [1¼ cups] dried chickpeas, soaked
in cold water overnight, then drained

1 fresh bay leaf

1 onion, halved widthways

1 bulb of garlic, halved widthways

2 sprigs of thyme, plus ¼ cup thyme leaves

1 small clove of garlic, crushed

Juice of 1 large lemon

1 fresh long green chilli,
seeded and finely chopped

1 bunch of purslane or watercress, picked

1 Lebanese cucumber, peeled, quartered
lengthways and cut into 1 cm pieces

½ small Spanish onion, finely chopped

½ cup each coarsely chopped
mint and flat-leaf parsley

1 Place ⅓ cup olive oil, 2 tsp sumac and paprika in a small bowl, season to taste and stir to combine. Place lamb fillets in a glass or ceramic bowl, pour sumac mixture over and turn to coat, then cover with plastic wrap and refrigerate for at least 2 hours.

2 Meanwhile, place chickpeas, bay leaf, onion, garlic bulb and thyme sprigs in a large saucepan, cover with water and bring to the boil, then simmer over low heat for 1¾-2 hours or until chickpeas are tender. Strain chickpeas and transfer to a large bowl, discarding liquid, bay leaf, onion, garlic and thyme.

3 Place garlic clove on a chopping board, sprinkle with ½ tsp sea salt and, using the back of a large knife, crush garlic until a smooth paste forms. Transfer garlic paste to a bowl, add lemon juice, chilli, remaining olive oil and sumac and stir to combine. Add dressing to warm chickpeas, season to taste and stir to combine, then cover with plastic wrap and leave to cool to room temperature.

4 Barbecue or char-grill drained lamb fillets over high heat, turning halfway through cooking, for 2-3 minutes for medium rare or until cooked to your liking. Cover with foil and stand for 5 minutes, then cut into thick slices on the diagonal.

5 Add remaining ingredients to chickpeas and toss gently to combine. Divide chickpea salad among plates or bowls, top with sliced lamb and serve immediately.

Serves 4-6

SOAKING CHICKPEAS

The following quick soaking method is an alternative to soaking chickpeas and other dried legumes overnight in cold water. Cook required quantity of chickpeas or dried beans in a large saucepan of rapidly boiling water for 2-3 minutes, then remove from heat and leave, covered, for 1 hour, drain and proceed with the recipe. Beans absorb warm water more rapidly. While the aim of soaking is to hydrate the beans, it is useful to note that there is a limit to the amount of water chickpeas and dried beans can absorb, so it is not necessary to soak beans for longer than between 4 to 8 hours, depending on the type of bean and how fresh it is. Fresher beans hydrate more quickly.

MIDDLE EASTERN PRAWNS WITH BARLEY TABBOULEH

Karen Martini – Chef, Melbourne Wine Room, Melbourne

150 ml extra-virgin olive oil

3 cloves of garlic, coarsely chopped

1 tbsp finely chopped preserved lemon [see page 74]

50 g sumac [see page 74]

¼ cup coriander seeds, dry-roasted and finely ground

2 tbsp cumin seeds, dry-roasted and finely ground

1 tbsp ground cinnamon

4 fresh small red chillies, thinly sliced

Juice of ½ lemon

16 large green king prawns, peeled and cleaned, leaving tails intact

1 cup Greek-style yoghurt

1 tbsp finely chopped preserved lemon rind

2 vine-ripened tomatoes, finely chopped

BARLEY TABBOULEH

400 g [2 cups] pearl barley

200 ml classic vinaigrette [see page 26]

Juice of 2 lemons

1½ tbsp cumin seeds, dry-roasted, combined with 1½ tbsp sea salt and ground in a mortar, using a pestle

½ bunch of flat-leaf parsley, leaves removed and torn

½ bunch of watercress, sprigs picked

1 large Spanish onion, finely chopped

2 celery hearts, leaves and hearts thinly sliced

½ bunch of coriander, leaves torn

1 Combine olive oil, garlic, preserved lemon, spices, chillies and 1 tsp sea salt in a bowl. Stand in a warm place for 15 minutes for flavours to infuse.

2 Fill a large saucepan with water, add lemon juice and 2 tsp sea salt and bring to the boil. Add prawns and cook for 1-2 minutes or until colour changes and prawns are just cooked through. Drain immediately, add to oil mixture, then marinate, covered with plastic wrap, for 1 hour.

3 For barley tabbouleh, cook barley in boiling water for 1 hour or until tender, then drain well and transfer to a bowl. Add vinaigrette, lemon juice and cumin mixture, combine well, then stir in remaining ingredients. Season to taste with freshly ground black pepper and mix well.

4 Combine yoghurt and chopped preserved lemon rind and season to taste.

5 To serve, spread yoghurt dressing around the outside of a large platter, place barley tabbouleh in the centre, then place drained prawns over the yoghurt dressing. Scatter with chopped tomatoes and drizzle with remaining marinade mixture.

Serves 8

I love salads… they are so versatile and, because they are made from beautiful fresh food, they are incredibly good for you. I would eat salad every day, from a simple green salad to refresh my palate after a great meal, to a perfectly ripe tomato in summer to accompany a pasta dish, or a composite salad of many ingredients, pulled together with extra-virgin olive oil and lemon, with a glass of wine to make a delicious fresh lunch.

Neil Perry

SALAD OF BRAISED BEETROOT, PEAS AND BEANS

Neil Perry – Rockpool, Sydney

2 beetroot [about 350g each], scrubbed well and cut into 8 wedges (or use baby beetroot)

500 g baby green beans, trimmed

125 g blanched whole almonds

6 fresh dates, halved and pitted

2 tbsp honey

Juice of 2 lemons

500 g podded green peas

CHERMOULA

1 Spanish onion, coarsely chopped

6 cloves of garlic, coarsely chopped

1 bunch of coriander, including stalks, coarsely chopped

1 bunch of flat-leaf parsley, including stalks, coarsely chopped

1 tbsp ground cumin

1 tbsp ground coriander

1 tbsp chilli powder

2 tsp ground turmeric

2 tsp sweet paprika

1½ tsp ras el hanout [see page 74]

Juice of 1 lemon

¾ cup olive oil

1 For chermoula, process all ingredients and 1½ tsp sea salt in a food processor until a soft paste forms. Makes about 2⅓ cups.

2 Combine beetroot, beans, almonds, dates and chermoula in a tagine or casserole and add 1 litre water or enough to just cover vegetables. Stir in honey and lemon juice and season to taste, then bring mixture to a simmer and cook over low-medium heat for 30 minutes. Add peas and cook for another 30 minutes or until vegetables are very soft. Transfer to a bowl or platter and serve at room temperature.

Serves 6-8 as an accompaniment or part of a Middle Eastern feast

FATTOUSH

1 cup olive oil

2 pieces of Lebanese bread, quartered

500 g grape tomatoes or small
   cherry tomatoes, halved

2 Lebanese cucumbers, finely chopped

1½ cups [loosely packed] flat-leaf
   parsley, coarsely chopped

1½ cups [loosely packed] mint
   leaves, coarsely chopped

1 red capsicum, seeded and finely chopped

4 radishes, halved and thinly sliced

4 green onions, thinly sliced

1 tbsp sumac

½ cup extra-virgin olive oil

2 tbsp lemon juice

1 Heat olive oil in a large saucepan over medium heat, and, when hot, add half the Lebanese bread and fry until golden, then drain on absorbent paper. Repeat with remaining bread.
2 Combine tomatoes, cucumber, parsley, mint, capsicum, radishes and green onions in a large bowl and stir to combine. Coarsely break Lebanese bread, toss with vegetable mixture, then sprinkle over sumac, drizzle with extra-virgin olive oil and lemon juice, and mix gently to combine. Serve immediately.
Serves 8

TABBOULEH

320 g [2 cups] coarse burghul [see page 74]

1 telegraph cucumber [about 560g],
   seeded and finely chopped

½ bunch spring onions [about 6],
   finely chopped, including green stems

1½ cups [loosely packed] dill, finely chopped

1½ cups flat-leaf [loosely packed]
   parsley, finely chopped

1½ cups [loosely packed] mint, finely chopped

1 cup extra-virgin olive oil

   Juice of 2 lemons

1 tsp ground Aleppo pepper
   [see Glossary, under Chilli], optional

You can chop herbs in a food processor to speed up the method. Tabbouleh improves the longer you allow it to marinate.

1 Place burghul in a large bowl, cover with cold water and leave for 30 minutes or until burghul swells, then drain in a colander. Turn out burghul onto a clean tea towel or piece of muslin and squeeze to remove any remaining water.
2 Transfer burghul to a large bowl, add remaining ingredients and Aleppo pepper, if using, then season to taste and stir to combine well. Refrigerate for at least 30 minutes for flavours to develop. Salad will keep refrigerated in an airtight container for up to 5 days.
Serves 6

PICKLED CAULIFLOWER

500 g cauliflower, cut into small florets
1 tbsp cumin seeds, coarsely crushed
1 cup white wine vinegar
1 tbsp finely chopped dill

1 Place cauliflower in a large bowl, sprinkle over 1 tbsp sea salt and toss to coat. Cover with plastic wrap and leave for 1 hour or until cauliflower softens and liquid is released.
2 Add crushed cumin seeds and white wine vinegar and stir to combine, then cover and marinate for at least 2 hours.
3 Stir in dill, then serve as part of a mezze plate. Pickled cauliflower will keep, covered with pickling liquid, in an airtight container in the refrigerator, for up to 1 month.
Serves 4 as a mezze

ROASTED CHERRY TOMATOES

500 g cherry tomatoes, halved
2 tsp sumac [see page 74]
2 tbsp extra-virgin olive oil
¼ cup [firmly packed] basil, finely chopped
¼ cup [firmly packed] oregano, finely chopped

1 Place tomatoes, sumac and olive oil in a roasting pan, season to taste and toss to combine, then roast at 180C for 20 minutes or until soft. Add chopped herbs and gently stir to combine. Serve tomatoes warm or at room temperature.
Serves 4 as a mezze

LABNA ROLLED WITH HERBS

1 kg Greek-style yoghurt
½ cup [firmly packed] flat-leaf parsley, finely chopped
½ cup [firmly packed] mint, finely chopped
Extra-virgin olive oil, to serve

1 Place yoghurt and 2 tsp sea salt in a bowl and stir to combine.
2 Line a colander with muslin, then spoon yoghurt mixture into colander and place over a bowl. Cover and refrigerate for 2 days to drain liquid.
3 Discard drained liquid, roll tablespoonfuls of drained yoghurt into balls, then roll in chopped herbs until evenly coated.
4 Serve labna drizzled with extra-virgin olive oil. Labna will keep, covered in extra-virgin olive oil, in an airtight container in the refrigerator for up to 1 week.
Serves 4 as a mezze

CLOCKWISE FROM TOP: PICKLED CAULIFLOWER; ROASTED CHERRY TOMATOES; LABNA ROLLED WITH HERBS

asian

The vivid flavours and brisk textures of Asian food translate naturally into appealing salads. Some balance meats or seafood with abundant vegetables for a lunch or dinner that leaves you feeling light and healthy. The vegetarian ones are designed to be part of an Asian vegetarian meal, or served with meats or seafood such as satays, Thai fish cakes or ready-cooked Chinese barbecued duck or pork. They also team well with many Western dishes, such as pan-fried or barbecued fish, barbecued or plain boiled prawns, barbecued calamari or octopus, pork chops, poached or grilled chicken, or grilled steak.

All vegetables are susceptible to their environment, and Asian ones are especially so, deteriorating very quickly once they are picked. In Asia, cooks buy vegetables on the day they will use them, but if that is not practical, buy only what you'll use within a day or two and store the vegetables and herbs in the refrigerator in an airtight container or in a paper bag loosely enclosed in a plastic bag.

asian ingredients

LEMONGRASS [1]
Use only the tender, white, inner part of the stem, which has a strong lemon flavour and aroma.

THAI BASIL [2]
Quite different from common or sweet basil, this herb has pungent aniseed-flavoured leaves.

POMELO [3]
Believed to be the ancestor of grapefruit, whose flavour it somewhat resembles, this largest of all citrus fruits is thick-skinned and sometimes slightly dry.

SNAKE BEANS [4]
Similar to ordinary green beans, but a little stronger in flavour.

JICAMA [5]
The root of a leguminous vine, jicama is used both raw and cooked, and is prized for its crispness.

GREEN PAPAYA [6]
Firm and pleasantly acid, this is good with seafood or rich meats such as pork.

BANANA BLOSSOM [7]
The tender heart of this large flower is a crisp salad ingredient and can also be steamed or added to a soup or stew.

**TURMERIC [8],
GINGER, GALANGAL [9]**
These juicy rhizomes are from three related tropical plants. Ginger and galangal have a similar, though not identical, flavour. Turmeric, mostly available dried and ground to a bright yellow powder, tastes warm and earthy.

SHALLOTS [10]
There are several varieties, but red Asian shallots with their sweeter flavour are commonly used in Asian cooking.

KAFFIR LIME LEAVES [11]
With a heady scent and flavour, these are quite different from ordinary lime leaves.

VIETNAMESE MINT [12]
Its flavour is rather like coriander, but more assertive.

BONITO FLAKES [KEZURI-BUSHI]
Finely shaved flakes of dried bonito, which is a dark, oily fish. It is used with konbu seaweed to make the Japanese stock, dashi.

DRIED SHRIMP
These tiny, salty morsels are sold in packets and are added to soups, sauces, stir-fries and salads.

FISH SAUCE
This salty, smelly brown liquid, made from fermented fish or prawns, is a magical seasoning and flavour enhancer.

**MUNG BEAN NOODLES,
RICE VERMICELLI, GREEN TEA SOBA**
Mung bean noodles, also known as glass noodles or cellophane noodles, are fine and transparent. Rice vermicelli come in thin threads or flat ribbons. Green tea soba are thin noodles made from buckwheat and powdered green tea.

SESAME OIL
Strongly flavoured oil of toasted sesame seeds.

SHRIMP PASTE [BLACHAN, TRASI]
A pungent paste made from salted, dried prawns left to ripen in humid heat. Despite its smell, it combines with spices to produce wonderful flavour.

SOY SAUCE
Good soy sauce is made by adding yeast to mixed soybeans and grain [usually wheat] and leaving them to ferment and mature for up to six months. Look for 'naturally brewed' on the label. Lesser soys are made in a few days via chemicals. Dark soy is thicker but less salty than light. Japanese soy [shoyu] is less salty than Chinese, while Japanese tamari is a dark soy made with rice. Indonesian kecap manis is sweet, in balance with saltiness.

TAMARIND PUREE
The acid pulp of a bean-like tropical fruit. Sold dried, in blocks, it is reconstituted by pouring boiling water over, leaving to cool, rubbing between the fingers until soft, then sieving to remove fibres and seeds.

BANANA BLOSSOM, CHICKEN AND JICAMA SALAD

400 g chicken breast fillets, skinned

2 cups chicken stock

½ tsp black peppercorns

2 banana blossoms
[about 900g each, see page 94]

Juice of 2 lemons

12 cooked king prawns, peeled and cleaned,
leaving tails intact, halved lengthways

1 jicama [yam bean], peeled and
cut into julienne [see page 94]

1 small carrot, cut into julienne

2 red Asian shallots or shallots, halved
lengthways and thinly sliced [see page 94]

⅓ cup [loosely packed] Vietnamese
mint leaves, torn [see page 94]

⅓ cup [loosely packed] small mint leaves, torn

Fried shallots, to serve [see Glossary]

LIME JUICE DRESSING

¼ cup lime juice

1½ tbsp fish sauce

2 tsp caster sugar

2 fresh red birdseye chillies, seeded
and finely chopped [see Glossary]

1 small clove of garlic, finely chopped

1 Place chicken, stock, peppercorns and 1 cup water in a saucepan, then slowly bring to the boil and simmer over medium heat for 8-10 minutes or until just cooked through. Remove chicken and set aside to cool, then tear into bite-size pieces.

2 For lime juice dressing, place all ingredients and 2 tbsp warm water in a bowl and stir to combine. Cover and set aside for flavours to develop. Makes about ⅓ cup.

3 Meanwhile, remove and reserve outer bracts from banana blossoms until pale inner section is revealed. Thinly slice the inner section widthways, place in a bowl of water with lemon juice and leave for 20 minutes, drain, then rinse with cold water. Place in cold water and leave for 15 minutes.

4 Place drained chopped banana blossom, chicken and remaining ingredients in a bowl, add dressing and toss to combine. Serve salad in reserved banana bracts, scattered with fried shallots.

Serves 4 as a light meal or 6-8 as part of an Asian-style banquet

VARIATION

✱ For a Vietnamese-style chicken 'coleslaw', combine shredded poached chicken with shredded Chinese cabbage, grated carrot and some thinly sliced coriander and mint. Scatter with chopped unsalted peanuts and toss with the lime juice dressing as above.

CHASOBA NOODLES WITH TRADITIONAL ACCOMPANIMENTS

400 g dried green tea
    soba noodles [see Glossary]
1 tsp sesame oil
40 g sesame seeds, roasted
1 sheet of nori [see Glossary]
4 green onions, finely chopped
3 cm piece of ginger, cut into julienne
    Wasabi paste, to serve

DIPPING SAUCE

1 tbsp bonito flakes
    [kezuri-bushi, see page 94]
⅓ cup shoyu [see page 94]
⅓ cup mirin [see Glossary]
½ tsp caster sugar

This cold, traditional Japanese summer dish is presented with individual bowls of various accompaniments that are added to the dipping sauce, according to the diner's palate. To eat, the sauce is held in one hand, while a little bunch of noodles, held between chopsticks, is dipped into the seasoned sauce. If preferred, the noodles can be tossed with the sauce.

1 Cook noodles in boiling water for 4 minutes or until al dente, drain and rinse under cold water, then drain well. Transfer to a bowl and toss with sesame oil and seeds. Carefully hold nori sheet, between tongs, over a medium gas flame for 1 minute or until roasted. Cool, then using kitchen scissors, cut into 2mm-wide strips.
2 For dipping sauce, combine all ingredients and 1½ cups water in a small saucepan and simmer for 5 minutes, remove from heat, cool, then strain through a fine sieve.
3 Pile noodles equally on plates, scatter with nori strips, then serve accompanied by individual bowls of dipping sauce, green onion, ginger and wasabi paste.
Serves 6 as a starter or light meal

TUNA TATAKI WITH PONZU SAUCE

100 g mizuna [see Glossary]
30 g Japanese rice seasoning [see Glossary]
6 yellow-fin tuna steaks [about 200g each]
    Steamed short-grain rice, to serve

PONZU SAUCE

⅓ cup lemon juice
⅓ cup lime juice
2 tbsp shoyu [see page 94, under Soy Sauce]
1 tsp finely grated ginger
2 tsp rice vinegar

1 For ponzu sauce, combine all ingredients in a small bowl. Makes about ¾ cup.
2 Place mizuna in a bowl, add half the ponzu sauce and toss to combine.
3 Place rice seasoning in a shallow bowl, then coat tuna steaks with seasoning, shaking to remove excess.
4 Barbecue tuna steaks on a flat plate over high heat for 1 minute on each side. Remove immediately and slice. Serve on top of steamed rice, with mizuna salad and remaining ponzu sauce passed separately.
Serves 6

CHASOBA NOODLES WITH
TRADITIONAL ACCOMPANIMENTS

CAMBODIAN BEEF SALAD

600 g piece of beef eye fillet

Fried shallots, to serve [see Glossary]

MARINADE

6 coriander roots and stems, rinsed and chopped

2 cloves of garlic, chopped

1 tbsp black peppercorns, dry-roasted and ground

1 tbsp light soy sauce

1 tbsp fish sauce

1 tbsp vegetable oil

LIME JUICE DRESSING

¼ cup lime juice

1½ tbsp fish sauce

2 tsp caster sugar

1-2 fresh red chillies, seeded and finely chopped

1 small clove of garlic, finely chopped

SALAD

1 Lebanese cucumber, sliced into ribbons with a vegetable peeler

½ mignonette lettuce, washed and leaves torn

½ butter lettuce, washed and leaves torn

125 g cherry tomatoes, halved

½ cup [loosely packed] coriander sprigs

¼ cup [loosely packed] Thai basil leaves, torn [see page 94]

¼ cup [loosely packed] mint leaves, torn

1 For marinade, process all ingredients in a small food processor or pound in a mortar, using a pestle, to a coarse paste. Place beef in a ceramic or glass dish, add marinade and rub over beef. Cover and refrigerate for at least 2 hours. Return beef to room temperature before cooking.

2 Barbecue beef on a flat plate over medium-high heat for 15-20 minutes, turning halfway through cooking, for medium rare or until cooked to your liking. Remove beef from heat, cover loosely with foil and rest for 10 minutes before serving.

3 Meanwhile, for lime juice dressing, combine all ingredients with 2 tbsp warm water in a small bowl and stir until sugar dissolves.

4 For salad, combine all ingredients on a platter or in a bowl. Just before serving, pour ¼ cup dressing over and toss to combine. Cut beef into thin slices and place on salad. Serve topped with fried shallots, with remaining dressing passed separately.

Serves 4 as a light meal or 6 as part of an Asian-style banquet

*A great dressing makes a salad three-dimensional. Different textures
from your ingredients are imperative to the salad being interesting.
I love how salads excite the palate and soul and are thoroughly good
for you. There is no substitute for fresh, quality ingredients.*

George Sinclair

SALAD OF KING PRAWNS, GREEN PAPAYA, SHALLOTS, LIME, PEANUTS, CHILLI AND MINT

George Sinclair – Yellow, Sydney

12	cooked king prawns, peeled and cleaned, leaving tails intact
100 g	cooked school prawns, heads removed
120 g	Chinese cabbage, cut into 1cm-wide strips
¼	green papaya, peeled and cut into julienne [see Glossary]
1½	cups [loosely packed] mixed herbs, including coriander, basil and mint leaves
50 g	ripe papaya, cut into 5mm pieces
50 g	roasted peanuts, coarsely chopped
1	cup [loosely packed] watercress sprigs
½ tsp	finely ground dried shrimp [see page 94]
20 g	[¼ cup] fried shallots [see Glossary]

LIME AND CHILLI DRESSING

4	cloves of garlic
4	fresh long red chillies, coarsely chopped
2 tbsp	grated palm sugar [see Glossary]
¼	cup fish sauce [see page 94]
2½ tbsp	freshly squeezed lemon juice
2½ tbsp	freshly squeezed lime juice

1 For lime and chilli dressing, place garlic and chillies in a mortar and, using a pestle, pound until a coarse paste forms. Add palm sugar, fish sauce and lemon and lime juices and combine well, adjusting taste with more sugar or fish sauce, if desired. Makes about ¾ cup.
2 Place remaining ingredients except fried shallots in a bowl, add ½ cup lime and chilli dressing and toss to combine well, then divide among bowls, scatter with fried shallots and serve immediately.
Serves 4

MISO PORK FILLETS WITH ASIAN LEAF AND NOODLE SALAD

2 small pork fillets [about 250g each]

1 tbsp red miso [see Glossary]

⅓ cup shoyu or other light soy sauce [see page 94]

2 tbsp vegetable oil

300 g dried gooksu noodles or other flat wheat flour noodles

100 g mizuna [see Glossary]

50 g snow pea shoots, trimmed

1 Lebanese cucumber, sliced into ribbons using a vegetable peeler

2 tbsp lemon juice

1 tsp rice vinegar

1 tbsp sesame seeds, roasted

Sesame oil, to serve

1 Place pork in a glass or ceramic dish, combine miso, 1 tbsp shoyu and 1 tbsp oil and spoon over pork, turning to coat evenly, then cover and refrigerate for at least 15 minutes. Heat remaining oil in an ovenproof frying pan, add pork and cook over high heat for 2-3 minutes or until evenly browned. Transfer to oven and roast at 220C for 10-12 minutes or until cooked to your liking, then remove pork and rest for 5 minutes. Cut into thin slices on the diagonal.
2 Meanwhile, cook noodles in boiling water for 3-4 minutes or until al dente, drain, refresh in iced water, then drain again and place in a large bowl with leaves and cucumber.
3 Combine remaining soy sauce, lemon juice and rice vinegar, then pour over leaves and noodles and toss gently to combine. Divide salad between 4 bowls, top with sliced pork and serve immediately, scattered with sesame seeds and drizzled with a little sesame oil.
Serves 4

GOOKSU NOODLES

In Korea, gooksu is the general term for noodles and also refers specifically to long, thin strips of noodles made from wheat flour, egg and water. Although they were traditionally homemade, now they are more commonly bought dried, in either round or flat versions. Flat gooksu noodles are usually stir-fried, while the round ones are often found in soups, such as the Korean specialty kalgooksu, an anchovy-based, chilli-laden dish. If gooksu noodles are not available, substitute with the same quantity of soba noodles or dried flat wheat noodles.

CHINESE ROAST DUCK, JICAMA, WATERCRESS AND MINT SALAD

1 Chinese roast duck

1 small jicama [about 285g,
    see page 94], peeled and shredded

100 g watercress sprigs or snow pea shoots

½ cup torn mint leaves

TAMARIND DRESSING

1 tbsp rice vinegar

1 tbsp tamarind purée [see page 94],
    combined with 1 tbsp water

1 tbsp fish sauce

3 tsp caster sugar

1 tsp finely grated ginger

1 For tamarind dressing, place all ingredients in a bowl and whisk to combine.
2 Remove meat and skin from duck and, using your fingers, shred and place in a bowl with remaining ingredients. Pour tamarind dressing over, toss gently to combine and serve immediately.
Serves 4 as a starter or light meal

GRILLED LEMONGRASS BEEF AND NOODLE PLATTER WITH NUOC CHAM

250 g dried rice vermicelli, soaked in
    warm water for 2 minutes and drained

2 cups [firmly packed] herbs,
    including Thai basil, spearmint,
    Vietnamese mint and coriander

Beansprouts, cucumber and carrot, cut into
    julienne, and butter leaf lettuce, to serve

12 bamboo skewers, soaked in water
    for 20 minutes

LEMONGRASS BEEF

¼ cup vegetable oil

1 tbsp soy sauce

2 stalks of lemongrass, finely chopped

3 cloves of garlic, finely chopped

2 tbsp fish sauce

1 tbsp caster sugar

1 fresh red birdseye chilli, finely chopped

800 g fillet of beef, cut into 2-3cm pieces

NUOC CHAM

¼ cup fish sauce

1 tbsp caster sugar

½ tbsp lime juice

1 fresh red birdseye chilli, or to taste,
    finely chopped [see Glossary]

½ clove of garlic, finely chopped

1 For lemongrass beef, combine all ingredients except beef in a bowl. Add beef and turn to coat in marinade, then cover and refrigerate for 30 minutes.
2 For nuoc cham, place all ingredients and ½ cup water in a small bowl and stir until sugar dissolves, then stand for 10 minutes to allow flavours to develop. Makes about ¾ cup.
3 Combine rice vermicelli, a little oil, herbs, beansprouts, cucumber and carrots, then place on a platter with lettuce.
4 Thread beef onto skewers, then barbecue or char-grill for 2 minutes on each side for medium or until cooked to your liking. Serve immediately with noodle platter and bowls of nuoc cham for dipping.
Serves 4

CHINESE ROAST DUCK, JICAMA,
WATERCRESS AND MINT SALAD

GADO GADO

600 g chat potatoes

2 baby savoy cabbages

1 bunch of baby carrots,
trimmed and scrubbed

1 bunch of snake beans [see page 94],
trimmed and cut into 5cm lengths

125g mung bean sprouts, tails removed

2 Lebanese cucumbers, halved
lengthways, seeded and cut
on the diagonal into thick slices

150 g packet small fried tofu puffs,
[see Glossary]

3 hard-boiled eggs, peeled and quartered

Indonesian prawn crackers [krupuk],
steamed jasmine rice, lime wedges
and fried shallots [see Glossary],
optional, to serve

COOKED PEANUT SAUCE

4 red Asian shallots [see page 94],
coarsely chopped

1 stalk of lemongrass, finely chopped

3 coriander roots, cleaned
and coarsely chopped

2 cloves of garlic, crushed

4 dried long red chillies, soaked
in boiling water for 10 minutes,
seeded and coarsely chopped

½ tsp shrimp paste

½ tsp each cumin seeds and ground coriander

400 ml can coconut cream

1 tbsp peanut oil

185 g [1¼ cups] peeled, unsalted
peanuts, lightly roasted and finely ground

1 tbsp grated dark palm sugar [see Glossary]

2 tsp each tamarind purée [see page 94]

1 For cooked peanut sauce, process shallots, lemongrass, coriander roots, garlic, chillies, shrimp paste, spices and ¼ cup coconut cream in a food processor until a smooth paste forms. Heat oil in a heavy-based frying pan, add spice paste and cook over medium heat for 5 minutes or until fragrant. Add remaining coconut cream, ground peanuts, palm sugar and tamarind purée, and stir to combine, then cook over low heat, stirring frequently, for another 5 minutes or until sauce thickens. Season to taste with sea salt, transfer to a bowl and keep warm. Makes about 2 cups.

2 Cook potatoes, cabbage, carrots and beans in boiling salted water until just tender, then refresh in iced water and drain. Cut potatoes in half and cabbages into wedges.

3 Place vegetables, tofu puffs, quartered eggs, prawn crackers and lime wedges on a large plate and scatter with fried shallots, if using, then serve immediately with cooked peanut sauce and steamed rice, passed separately.

Serves 6

Being inspired by the visual feast at a market and then creating a tasty salad dish, with few ingredients and a well seasoned dressing – that to me makes a good salad.

Martin Boetz

STEAMED PIPI SALAD WITH BASIL AND GREEN CHILLI NAHM JIM

Martin Boetz – Longrain, Sydney

1 kg pipis or clams [vongole],
  soaked in cold water for 2 hours

1 cup [firmly packed] Thai basil leaves

½ cup [firmly packed] coriander leaves

5 cm piece of ginger,
  peeled and cut into julienne

4 kaffir lime leaves, thinly shredded

1 stalk of lemongrass,
  white part only, thinly sliced

2 fresh long green chillies,
  seeded and cut into julienne

1 fresh long red chilli,
  seeded and cut into julienne

GREEN CHILLI NAHM JIM

2 cloves of garlic

3 coriander roots,
  washed and scraped clean

3 fresh green birdseye
  chillies, coarsely chopped

3 fresh long green chillies,
  seeded and coarsely chopped

3 cm piece of galangal [see page 94],
  peeled and finely chopped

60g grated light palm sugar,
  or to taste [see Glossary]

¼ cup fish sauce [see page 94], or to taste

200 ml lime juice, or to taste

1 For green chilli nahm jim, place garlic, coriander roots, chillies and galangal in a mortar and, using a pestle, pound to a smooth paste. Add palm sugar and fish sauce and pound to combine, then add lime juice and stir to combine. Taste the nahm jim: the flavour should be a balance of sweet, sour, salty and hot. Add a little more palm sugar, fish sauce or lime juice if necessary. Makes about 1¼ cups.

2 Steam pipis over a saucepan of boiling water just until shells open, transfer to a bowl to cool, discarding unopened shells. Add nahm jim to cooled pipis and stir to combine. Pipis can be covered and refrigerated for up to 2 hours.

3 Add remaining ingredients, toss gently to combine, then divide among plates and serve immediately.

Serves 4-6

VIETNAMESE-STYLE LOTUS STEM AND PRAWN SALAD

Tony Tan – chef, food writer, food historian

500 g pickled lotus stems [see Glossary]

200 g cooked and sliced lotus root

16 large cooked king prawns, peeled and cleaned

½ red capsicum, cut into julienne

1 tbsp caster sugar

1 tbsp lime juice

1 cup [loosely packed] coriander leaves

½ cup [loosely packed] Vietnamese mint leaves [see page 94]

½ cup [loosely packed] dill sprigs

½ cup fried shallots [see Glossary]

NUOC CHAM

¼ cup fish sauce [see page 94]

1 tbsp caster sugar

½ tbsp lime juice

1 fresh red birdseye chilli, or to taste, finely chopped [see Glossary]

½ clove of garlic, finely chopped

1 For nuoc cham, place all ingredients and ½ cup water in a small bowl and stir until sugar dissolves, then stand for 10 minutes to allow flavours to develop.

2 Place all ingredients and 2 tbsp nuoc cham in a large bowl and toss gently to combine. Transfer salad to a large plate and serve immediately.

Serves 8 as part of an Asian-style banquet

LOTUS ROOT

While all parts of the lotus plant are used in cooking, including the stamens, leaves and flowers, the root is the most commonly consumed part. These edible rhizomes grow under water in ponds and lakes. Greyish-brown in colour, lotus roots are characterised by the lacy pattern of holes that become visible when a cross section is cut. They are prized in Asian cuisines for their crunchy texture, timid flavour and starchy consistency and are commonly paired with rich meats due to their ability to absorb oil. Lotus root is generally available from Asian greengrocers; when buying, choose those without decayed spots.

CRAB AND GLASS NOODLE SALAD WITH POMELO DRESSING

250 g mung bean vermicelli [see page 94]

1 pomelo, peeled, segmented, seeded and broken into bite-size pieces [see Glossary]

400 g cooked crabmeat

¼ cup [firmly packed] Vietnamese mint leaves [see Glossary]

⅓ cup [firmly packed] coriander leaves

100 g sprigs of watercress [about 1 bunch, picked]

POMELO DRESSING

⅓ cup pomelo juice [see Glossary]

1½ tbsp fish sauce

2 tsp caster sugar

2 fresh small red chillies, seeded and chopped

1 For pomelo dressing, combine all ingredients in a small bowl, stir until sugar dissolves, then cover and set aside.

2 Place vermicelli in a large heatproof bowl, cover with boiling water and soak for 3-4 minutes or until just soft, then drain, refresh in iced water and drain again.

3 Just before serving, place all ingredients in a large bowl, add dressing and toss gently to combine.

Serves 4 as a light meal or as part of an Asian-style banquet

CRAB, COCONUT AND CORIANDER SALAD

450 g blue swimmer or spanner crab meat

Flesh of 1 young coconut, thinly sliced [see Glossary]

1 shallot, finely chopped

1 Lebanese cucumber, seeded and finely chopped

½ cup [firmly packed] coriander leaves, torn

¼ cup [firmly packed] mint leaves, coarsely chopped

2 butter lettuces, outside leaves discarded, washed and small leaves trimmed

Sprigs of watercress and small red witlof leaves, optional, to serve

COCONUT DRESSING

1½ tbsp coconut vinegar [see Glossary]

1½ tbsp lime juice

3 tsp fish sauce

2 tsp caster sugar, or to taste

3 fresh small red chillies, seeded and finely chopped

1 For coconut dressing, combine all ingredients in a small bowl and stir until sugar dissolves. Place crabmeat, coconut flesh, shallot, cucumber and herbs in a large bowl, add dressing and toss gently to combine.

2 Serve spoonfuls of crab, coconut and coriander salad in lettuce cups, topped with watercress sprigs, with red witlof leaves to the side, if using. For a themed occasion, serve in small takeaway containers with chopsticks.

Serves 6 as a starter

CRAB AND GLASS NOODLE SALAD WITH POMELO DRESSING

This is a very easy and wonderfully fragrant salad. The components – fresh and dried herbs and spices, coconut, dried shrimp and fish – move it beyond an ordinary rice salad to being something truly gastronomic. It's nutritious and it appeals to all the senses. Eating it is like being in a tropical garden.

Tony Tan

MALAY NONYA RICE SALAD

Tony Tan – chef, food writer, food historian

150 g flathead fillets, skinned and pin-boned

⅓ cup vegetable oil

2 tbsp dried shrimp, soaked in boiling water for 10 minutes, drained and coarsely chopped [see Glossary]

700 g [3½ cups] steamed jasmine rice [about 240g uncooked], cooled

1 stalk of lemongrass, white part only, thinly sliced

4 snake beans, finely chopped [see Glossary]

3 red Asian shallots, thinly sliced

2-3 cm piece of fresh turmeric, peeled and thinly sliced [see Glossary]

45 g [½ cup] desiccated coconut, roasted

5 kaffir lime leaves, thinly sliced [see Glossary]

½ cup [loosely packed] Vietnamese mint, thinly sliced [see page 94]

½ cup [loosely packed] Thai basil leaves, thinly sliced [see page 94]

½ cup water celery (selom leaves), thinly sliced [see Glossary]

1 small Lebanese cucumber, seeded and finely chopped

The recipe for this aromatic salad from north Malaysia is adapted from the kitchens of the Mandarin Oriental Hotel in Kuala Lumpur.

1 Rub fish with 2 tsp sea salt, then heat oil in a frying pan, add fish and cook over medium-high heat for 5 minutes or until golden. Drain fish on absorbent paper, cool, then flake into small pieces and place in a large bowl.

2 Add soaked shrimp, rice, lemongrass, snake beans, shallots, turmeric, coconut and a pinch of caster sugar, then season to taste and combine gently. Fold in herbs, water celery and cucumber, then transfer salad to a large bowl or plate and serve immediately.

Serves 4-6 as part of an Asian banquet

meat

The salads in this chapter balance vegetable power with the savour and satisfaction of meat. They add up to the way we want to eat today – light-feeling but full of big flavours and good textures. They are all great party dishes and good for family meals, too – no more trouble than the standard meat and three veg. Try the warm ones for winter as well as summer – any one of them could be a triumphant surprise at a winter dinner party.

As with all salads, you can do much of the preparation hours or even a day ahead: prepare the vegetables, make sauces and dressings, marinate the meat for the two lamb salads, crumb the meat for the pork, grapefruit and avocado salad, and make the tuna mayonnaise for vitello tonnato. And you can be relaxed about the temperature at which you serve the meat – in fact, warm works better than piping hot for the warm salads, while carpaccio and vitello tonnato will be perfect if you cover and chill them ahead of time, then take them out of the refrigerator half an hour or so before serving, to allow the flavours time to come back to their fullest.

VITELLO TONNATO

600 g fillet of veal

Olive oil

Deep-fried capers
and crusty bread, to serve

TUNA MAYONNAISE

2 egg yolks

1 tsp Dijon mustard

1 cup grapeseed oil or olive oil

95 g can of tuna in brine, drained

2 tbsp lemon juice, or to taste

2 tbsp baby capers

2 tbsp finely chopped chives

1 Brush veal with olive oil and season to taste. Heat an ovenproof frying pan over high heat until hot, then add veal and cook, turning frequently, until browned all over. Transfer veal to a 200C oven and roast for 15 minutes or until nearly cooked through, then cool.

2 For tuna mayonnaise, process egg yolks and mustard in a food processor until well combined, then, with motor running, gradually add oil, drop by drop at first, then in a thin, steady stream until thick and emulsified. Add tuna and lemon juice and process until smooth. Add capers and chives and process until just combined, then season to taste. Makes about 1½ cups.

3 Thinly slice veal and place, overlapping, in the centre of 4 plates, spoon tuna mayonnaise over and sprinkle with fried capers. Serve with crusty bread passed separately.

Serves 4 as a starter

PORCHETTA WITH SPINACH SALAD

1.7 kg pork belly

10 cloves of garlic

1 cup [loosely packed] rosemary leaves

2 tbsp thyme leaves

1 tbsp dried chilli flakes

Lemon wedges, to serve

SPINACH SALAD

500 g spinach [about 2 bunches], trimmed

4 green onions, trimmed
and coarsely chopped

⅓ cup olive oil

Juice of 1 lemon

1 Using a sharp knife, score pork skin at 4cm intervals. Place 2 tbsp sea salt, garlic, herbs and chilli flakes in a food processor and pulse until coarsely chopped, or pound in a mortar using a pestle. Place pork, skin-side down, on a work surface and sprinkle salt mixture evenly over meat.

2 Roll up meat widthways and secure tightly with kitchen string at regular intervals. Place pork in a lightly oiled roasting pan, then rub 2 tsp sea salt into skin. Roast at 240C for 20 minutes, turning once, then reduce temperature to 160C, cover with foil and cook for another 3 hours or until tender. Remove pork from pan, cool, then cover and refrigerate until ready to serve. Pork will keep refrigerated for up to 1 week.

3 For spinach salad, cook spinach and green onions in a saucepan of boiling salted water for 15-20 minutes or until well cooked. Drain and cool, then place in a bowl with oil and lemon juice, season to taste and combine well. Serve porchetta, thinly sliced, with spinach salad and lemon wedges to the side.

Serves 6-8

CRUMBED PORK, RUBY GRAPEFRUIT AND AVOCADO SALAD WITH CHIVE VINAIGRETTE

4 pork leg steaks

Plain flour, seasoned to taste

2 eggs, lightly beaten with 1 tbsp milk

140 g [2 cups] fresh breadcrumbs
made from day-old bread

Olive oil

2 ruby grapefruit, peeled and segmented
over a bowl, to reserve juice

2 baby cos, leaves separated
and cut into 4cm slices

2 avocados, halved, seeded,
peeled and cut into 1cm-thick slices

CHIVE VINAIGRETTE

2 tsp Dijon mustard

2 tsp sherry vinegar

1 tbsp reserved ruby grapefruit juice

⅓ cup extra-virgin olive oil

¼ cup finely chopped chives [about 1 bunch]

1 For chive vinaigrette, combine mustard, vinegar and grapefruit juice in a small bowl and gradually whisk in olive oil until well combined and emulsified. Season to taste and stir in chives just before serving.

2 Using the flat side of a meat mallet, pound pork steaks until about 5mm thick. Dust pork with seasoned flour, shake off excess, dip in beaten egg mixture, then dip in breadcrumbs, pressing firmly to coat. Heat just enough olive oil to cover the base of a heavy-based frying pan and cook pork, in batches, over medium heat for 2 minutes on each side or until crisp and cooked through. Drain on absorbent paper, then cut into 3-4cm strips.

3 Combine grapefruit segments, sliced cos, avocado and chive vinaigrette in a bowl and toss gently to combine. Add sliced pork, toss gently, then divide among 4 plates and serve immediately.

Serves 4 as a light meal

BREADCRUMBS

It is best to use day-old bread when making breadcrumbs for coating food that is to be fried, because its drier texture makes finer, more uniform crumbs than those made with fresh bread. Not only do finer crumbs adhere to the coated food more easily, they also coat it more evenly and are crisper when cooked. Use good quality bread such as sourdough or ciabatta for making crumbs, as highly processed bread contains more sugar and preservatives and burns more easily. It is also recommended that day-old bread be used in preference to stale bread, which can give the crumbs an undesirable taste. The better the flavour of the bread, the better the crumbs will taste.

AMERICAN-STYLE PORK RIBS IN BARBECUE SAUCE WITH BLACK-EYE BEAN, CORN AND CORIANDER SALAD

Sunflower oil

3 cloves of garlic, finely chopped

1 tbsp sweet Spanish paprika

3 tsp mustard powder

½ tsp celery seeds

¼ tsp each ground mace, chilli powder, ground allspice, ground cloves and ground ginger

Large pinch of smoked Spanish paprika

2 tbsp cider vinegar

50 g [¼ cup, firmly packed] dark brown sugar

700 ml passata [see Glossary]

½ cup dry apple cider

¼ cup Worcestershire sauce

1.5 kg pork ribs

BLACK-EYE BEAN, CORN AND CORIANDER SALAD

2 corn cobs, husks and silks removed

370 g [2 cups] black-eye beans, soaked in cold water overnight, rinsed and drained, then cooked in boiling water for 40 minutes or until tender

2 fresh long red chillies, seeded and finely chopped

1 bunch of chives, chopped

⅓ cup chopped coriander

2 tbsp lime juice

¼ cup extra-virgin olive oil

1 Heat 2 tbsp oil in a saucepan, add garlic and cook for 30 seconds, then add sweet paprika, mustard powder, celery seeds, spices and smoked paprika, and cook for another 30 seconds or until fragrant. Add vinegar and cook for 1 minute or until reduced, then add remaining ingredients, except pork ribs, bring to the boil and simmer over low-medium heat for 20 minutes or until reduced to a thick sauce consistency. Reserve ½ cup sauce for serving, then transfer remaining sauce to a shallow ceramic or glass dish large enough to contain pork ribs, and cool completely.

2 Cut ribs into sections of about 3-4 ribs each, then add to cooled barbecue sauce, cover and refrigerate for at least 2 hours or overnight.

3 Meanwhile, for black-eye bean, corn and coriander salad, cook corn in boiling water for 5 minutes or until just tender. Drain and pat corn dry with absorbent paper, then barbecue, turning frequently, on a flat plate over high heat for 15 minutes or until kernels are slightly charred. Remove and cool. Stand 1 cob at a time on its end and, using a small sharp knife, remove kernels by cutting downwards as close to the cob as possible.

4 Combine corn kernels, drained black-eye beans and remaining ingredients in a large bowl, season to taste, then toss gently.

5 Remove ribs from marinade, reserving marinade, then barbecue on a grill plate over medium-high heat for 15 minutes, brushing frequently with reserved marinade and turning halfway through cooking, or until well browned and just cooked through. Serve immediately with black-eye bean, corn and coriander salad, with reserved barbecue sauce passed separately.

Serves 6

I find there's nothing more tempting than a salad with a touch of spice for extra flavour. In this lamb salad, the cumin works with the lamb to create a true taste and sense of the exotic. This balances with the feta and the sugars of the sweet potato and honey. It is the type of salad I love to serve during the summer months – great for a relaxed Sunday afternoon lunch at home.

Matt Moran

SPICED LAMB SALAD WITH SWEET POTATO AND MUSTARD SEED DRESSING

Matt Moran – Aria, Sydney

Extra-virgin olive oil
1 tbsp cumin seeds, dry-roasted and finely ground
Finely grated rind of 1 lemon
3 cloves of garlic, finely chopped
1 tbsp chopped rosemary leaves
2 fresh bay leaves, torn
1 kg lamb fillets, trimmed
2 orange sweet potatoes [about 740g]
2 bunches of asparagus
250 g cherry tomatoes, halved
200 g rocket leaves
150 g soft marinated goat's feta

MUSTARD SEED DRESSING

1 tbsp yellow mustard seeds
25 ml chardonnay vinegar
1½ tbsp honey
1½ tbsp Dijon mustard
1 clove of garlic, crushed
½ tsp grated ginger
2 tsp lemon juice
100 ml extra-virgin olive oil
2½ tbsp vegetable oil

1 Combine 2 tbsp olive oil, cumin, lemon rind, garlic, rosemary and bay leaves in a glass or ceramic dish, add lamb and turn to coat in mixture, then cover and refrigerate for 2-4 hours or overnight.

2 Meanwhile, for mustard seed dressing, soak mustard seeds in vinegar for 1 hour, then add 1½ tbsp water and remaining ingredients, except oils, and whisk to combine. Gradually add combined olive and vegetable oils and whisk until well combined, then season to taste. Makes about 1 cup.

3 Cook unpeeled sweet potatoes in boiling salted water for 20-30 minutes or until tender, then drain and cool. Remove skins and cut into 2cm-thick rounds. Heat 2 tbsp olive oil in a heavy-based frying pan and cook sweet potato, in batches, for 1-2 minutes on each side or until golden, then drain on absorbent paper.

4 Cook asparagus in boiling salted water until just tender, drain, refresh in iced water, then drain again. Combine sweet potatoes, asparagus, tomatoes and rocket on a large platter and set aside.

5 Meanwhile, heat a little olive oil in a frying pan and pan-fry lamb fillets for 2 minutes on each side for medium rare or until cooked to your liking. Season to taste, then rest lamb for 5 minutes before cutting each fillet into 3 on the diagonal. Place over vegetables on platter and scatter with feta. Drizzle salad with dressing and serve immediately.

Serves 6-8

This is a satisfying, warm salad for the winter months using blood sausage, a delicious product that is underutilised in Australia and yet extensively eaten in Europe.

Janni Kyritsis

STEAMED BABY POTATOES WITH BLOOD SAUSAGE AND CRISP PARSLEY

Janni Kyritsis – chef

1.5 kg small kipfler or charlotte potatoes, scrubbed

175g butter, chopped

1 cup [firmly packed] flat-leaf parsley leaves

500 g French- or Spanish-style blood sausages, casings removed, coarsely crumbled

1 Steam potatoes, in batches, if necessary, over a saucepan of simmering water until tender. Place in a large bowl with 50g butter, season to taste, toss gently and keep warm.
2 Melt remaining butter in a large heavy-based frying pan, add parsley when just foaming and cook over high heat for 1-2 minutes or until just crisp. Strain parsley and butter through a sieve over a bowl, reserve the butter, then drain parsley on absorbent paper and season to taste.
3 Heat reserved butter in same pan, add crumbled sausage and cook over medium heat for 3-4 minutes or until warmed through. Place potatoes in a large shallow bowl, then spoon blood sausage over and scatter with crisp parsley.
Serves 8-10 as an accompaniment

BEEF CARPACCIO WITH PIQUANT SAUCE AND LEMON SALSA

850 g piece of beef topside,
cut into 2 mm-thick slices

PIQUANT SAUCE

2 egg yolks

2 tsp Dijon mustard

300 ml olive oil

Worcestershire sauce
and Tabasco sauce, to taste

LEMON SALSA

½ bunch of flat-leaf parsley, picked

2 lemons, rind and pith removed, segmented

100 g [¼ cup] caper flowers
preserved in oil, drained [see Glossary]

2 tbsp extra-virgin olive oil

1 For piquant sauce, process egg yolks, mustard and a pinch of sea salt in a food processor until well combined, then, with motor running, gradually add oil in a thin, steady stream until mixture is thick and emulsified. Season to taste with freshly ground white pepper, Worcestershire sauce and Tabasco, then stir in 2 tbsp boiling water or enough to achieve the desired consistency. Makes about 1½ cups.

2 For lemon salsa, combine all ingredients in a small bowl and stand at room temperature until required.

3 Divide meat in a single layer among 6 plates, drizzle with piquant sauce, top with a little lemon salsa and serve immediately.

Serves 6 as a starter or light meal

VEAL CARPACCIO WITH RUBY GRAPEFRUIT AND CELERY SALAD

One at a time, place twelve 1 cm-thick slices of veal girello [eye of round] between pieces of plastic wrap and, using the flat side of a meat mallet, pound until paper-thin. Using a mandolin or large sharp knife, thinly slice 1 celery heart lengthways and 2 spring onions widthways, then combine in a bowl with segments of 2 ruby grapefruit. Place 2 tsp celery seeds, ½ tsp cumin seeds and 1 tsp dried chilli flakes in a mortar, and using a pestle, pound until finely crushed, then add 1 tbsp sea salt and combine well. Place veal in a single layer on 6 plates, top with ruby grapefruit and celery salad, sprinkle with spice mixture and drizzle with extra-virgin olive oil. Serve immediately.
Serves 6 as a starter or light meal.

GOAN MASALA LAMB CUTLETS WITH KACHUMBER SALAD

¼ tsp black peppercorns, dry-roasted

1 tsp cumin seeds, dry-roasted

2 tsp coriander seeds, dry-roasted

1 tsp each ground turmeric and garam masala

¼ tsp ground cloves

3 cloves of garlic, crushed

2 tsp grated ginger

1 fresh long green chilli, seeded and finely chopped

1 tsp muscovado sugar [see Glossary]

1 tbsp tamarind purée [see Glossary]

¼ cup coconut milk

Juice of 1 lime

12 french-trimmed lamb cutlets [about 40g each, see Glossary]

Char-grilled parathas or chapatis and lime wedges, to serve

KACHUMBER SALAD

¼ tsp ground cumin

Pinch of chilli powder

1 tbsp lime juice, or to taste

1 tbsp vegetable oil

2 vine-ripened tomatoes, cut into thin wedges

1 small Lebanese cucumber, halved lengthways, then thinly sliced on the diagonal

½ small Spanish onion, very thinly sliced

¼ cup coriander leaves, torn

¼ tsp black mustard seeds

1 Place peppercorns, cumin and coriander seeds in a mortar and, using a pestle, grind to a fine powder. Process ground spices and remaining ingredients except lamb in a food processor until a smooth paste forms, then pour over lamb in a flat ceramic or glass dish, stirring to coat well. Cover and refrigerate for at least 2 hours or overnight.

2 For kachumber salad, place cumin, chilli, lime juice and oil in a small bowl, season to taste and stir to combine. Place tomatoes, cucumber, onion and coriander in a bowl and, just before serving, add dressing and mustard seeds and toss to combine.

3 Remove lamb from marinade, leaving some marinade on cutlets. Season to taste with sea salt, then char-grill for 2-3 minutes on each side for medium rare or until cooked to your liking. Cover and rest in a warm place for 5 minutes.

4 Serve cutlets with kachumber salad and char-grilled parathas or chapatis and lime wedges, passed separately.

Serves 4

poultry & game

Who doesn't love a chicken salad, and what cook doesn't love to find a great new one? Casual or elegant, divinely cool or warm and luscious, delightful for one or two, perfect for a crowd, popular with all ages, it's right for all types of occasions, from an easy weekend lunch to a wedding.

Just be sure of two important points. The chicken must be juicy and flavoursome, so buy the best you can afford – certainly free-range, aim for organic. And if you're poaching breasts, as you often are for a salad, keep a close eye on them as they'll quickly turn dry and tough if overcooked. Cover them with cold water, bring just to a bare simmer and cook on low heat until the meat feels springy when you push it with your finger. Cool and store in the cooking liquid.

Salads are also a wonderfully relaxed way to present those other choice birds – quail, guinea fowl and pheasant. Rich chicken livers make a sophisticated little warm salad. And we've included a brilliant recipe for that now-fashionable game meat, rabbit, and an attractive way for the Christmas turkey to take another bow as a fresh-tasting Boxing Day salad.

RABBIT RILLETTES

1.7 kg farmed white rabbit

750 g pork belly meat,
cut into 2cm pieces

150 g pork fat

125 ml dry white wine

1 clove of garlic, bruised

3 sprigs of thyme

Cornichons, to serve
[see Glossary]

The leanness of rabbit meat means it can be dry – a problem which is overcome when used in confit or its derivation, rillettes. From the French word 'rille', meaning slice, rillettes are made from shredded confit meat such as rabbit, pork, goose or duck with added herbs, which are then stored in fat.

1 Using a sharp knife, remove forequarters, legs and loins from rabbit and place in a large bowl with pork belly. Add 2 tbsp sea salt, stir to combine, then cover and refrigerate overnight.
2 Place rabbit pieces, pork, pork fat, white wine, garlic and thyme in a large casserole, then cook, covered, at 150C for 3 hours.
3 Strain meat through a fine sieve over a bowl and reserve fat. Using 2 forks, finely shred meat and season to taste with freshly ground black pepper. Transfer meat to a 1-litre-capacity sterilised glass or ceramic jar and pour over reserved strained fat, then cool and seal. Rabbit rillettes will keep, sealed and stored in the refrigerator, for up to 3 months.
4 Bring required quantity of rillettes to room temperature before serving. Serve with toasted baguette or sourdough bread and cornichons to the side.
Makes 4 cups

BABY ENDIVE, HAZELNUT AND RABBIT RILLETTES SALAD WITH SPICED PRUNES

1 cup aged red wine vinegar

2½ tbsp granulated sugar

1 stick of cinnamon

8 cloves

250 g [1½ cups] pitted prunes

¼ cup extra-virgin olive oil

2 tsp Dijon mustard

2 shallots, peeled and finely chopped

480 g baby endive leaves
[about 2 heads], trimmed and washed

75 g [½ cup] hazelnuts, roasted,
peeled and coarsely chopped

180 g [1 cup] room temperature rabbit
rillettes [recipe above], broken
into bite-size pieces with a fork

1 Place red wine vinegar, sugar, cinnamon and cloves in a saucepan and stir continuously over low heat until sugar dissolves. Place prunes in a heatproof bowl and pour spiced vinegar over. Cool to room temperature, then set aside for at least 6 hours, or up to 1 week, to allow flavours to develop. Spiced prunes will keep in an airtight container in the refrigerator for up to 6 months.
2 Remove 2 tbsp spiced vinegar from prunes and place in a screw-top jar with olive oil, mustard and shallots. Shake to combine.
3 Slice prunes in half lengthways, then place in a large bowl with baby endive, hazelnuts and rillettes and toss gently to combine. Divide salad among 4 plates, drizzle over a little dressing and serve immediately.
Serves 4

BABY ENDIVE, HAZELNUT AND RABBIT RILLETTES SALAD WITH SPICED PRUNES

PERSIAN QUAIL, FIG AND POMEGRANATE SALAD

1 shallot, finely chopped

1 tsp sumac [see Glossary]

½ tsp ground cinnamon

1 tbsp pomegranate molasses [see Glossary]

⅓ cup extra-virgin olive oil

4 jumbo quail [about 200g each], butterflied (see note below)

Olive oil

1 piece of Lebanese bread

1 radicchio, outer leaves discarded, washed

½ cup [firmly packed] basil leaves

¼ cup [firmly packed] flat-leaf parsley leaves

50 g [½ cup] walnut halves, roasted

6 ripe black figs, quartered lengthways

120 g sheep's milk feta, crumbled

½ pomegranate, seeds removed and pith discarded

1 Combine shallot, sumac, cinnamon, a pinch of caster sugar, pomegranate molasses and extra-virgin olive oil in a small bowl, season to taste and whisk to combine well. Place quail in a glass or ceramic bowl, add half the dressing, combine well, cover and refrigerate for 4 hours or overnight.

2 Heat 2 tbsp olive oil in a heavy-based frying pan and cook quail, in batches, skin-side down, for 4-5 minutes over medium heat or until golden, then transfer quail to an oven tray, skin-side up, and cook at 180C for 5-6 minutes or until breasts are just cooked but still slightly pink. Transfer to a warm place to rest for 10 minutes, then cut each quail in half along the breastbone and cut in half again between legs and breasts to give 4 pieces.

3 Lightly brush bread on each side with olive oil, place on an oven tray, then bake at 180C for 8-10 minutes or until crisp and golden. Cool, then break into large pieces.

4 Tear radicchio leaves into large pieces and place in a bowl with basil, parsley, walnuts, figs, toasted bread, quail, feta, pomegranate seeds and remaining dressing. Combine well, place in 4 bowls and serve immediately.

Serves 4

BUTTERFLYING QUAIL

The term 'butterfly' in cooking means to split down the centre, cutting almost but not completely through. The two halves are then opened, and generally pressed flat in order to resemble a butterfly shape. To butterfly quail, use a heavy knife or poultry shears to cut through either side of the backbone. Discard the bone, then open the quail, flesh-side up, on a work surface, and, using your hands, press on the breastbone to flatten the quail completely. In this shape, the quail will be more evenly coated in the marinade and will also cook more evenly, giving a crispier skin all over.

BRAISED GUINEA FOWL SALAD

Extra-virgin olive oil
10 g butter
1.1 kg guinea fowl
125 ml dry white wine
8 cloves of garlic, unpeeled
2 sprigs of rosemary
2 sprigs of thyme
1 bunch of baby beetroot, trimmed and washed
8 asparagus spears, trimmed
175 g baby green beans, trimmed
50 g baby spinach
2 tsp balsamic vinegar

1 Heat 2 tbsp olive oil and butter in a large non-stick frying pan, add guinea fowl and cook over high heat until browned all over. Remove guinea fowl from pan and transfer to a heavy-based saucepan. Add wine to frying pan and stir to remove cooked pieces from base of pan, then pour over guinea fowl, add garlic and herbs, season to taste, cover and cook over low heat for 30 minutes. Remove pan from heat and stand, covered, for 15 minutes.

2 Remove guinea fowl from pan, cut down either side of backbone and discard bone, then cut in half through breastbone. Cut each piece of guinea fowl in half again, remove legs and thighs from each half in one piece, then remove breast fillets with wing attached, to give 4 pieces.

3 Remove, peel and reserve garlic, then strain pan juices through a fine sieve and season to taste.

4 Meanwhile, wrap beetroot in foil and roast at 200C for 45 minutes or until tender. Remove foil and, when cool enough, peel. Cut in half if large.

5 Blanch asparagus and beans in boiling salted water for 1 minute, drain, refresh in iced water, then drain again.

6 Combine spinach, asparagus, beans, garlic cloves and beetroot, then toss with balsamic vinegar and 1 tbsp olive oil and season to taste. To serve, divide salad among 4 plates, top with a piece of guinea fowl and drizzle with reserved pan juices.

Serves 4 as a light meal

DUCK, ORANGE, PINK GRAPEFRUIT AND WALNUT SALAD

4 duck breasts [about 150g each]
Olive oil

75 g (¾ cup) walnut halves

3 oranges, peeled, segmented
over a bowl, to reserve juices

2 pink grapefruit, peeled and segmented

1 baby endive, washed
and cut into 5cm lengths

1 radicchio, outer leaves discarded,
washed and cut into quarters

2 small yellow or red witlof, leaves
separated, large leaves halved

ORANGE VINCOTTO DRESSING

2 shallots, finely chopped

1 tbsp sherry vinegar

2 tbsp orange vincotto [see Glossary]

2 tbsp reserved orange juice

¼ cup extra-virgin olive oil

1 tbsp walnut oil

1 Trim excess duck fat from breasts, then score the skin and season to taste. Place 1 tsp olive oil in a large heavy-based frying pan, add duck skin-side down, then cook over medium heat for 8-10 minutes or until skin is golden and fat is rendered. Turn breasts over and cook for another 6-8 minutes. Remove duck from pan and keep warm.
2 Heat ½ cup olive oil in a heavy-based frying pan, add walnuts and cook over medium heat for 4 minutes or until walnuts are toasted. Using a slotted spoon, remove walnuts and drain on absorbent paper.
3 For orange vincotto dressing, combine all ingredients and season to taste. Makes about ¾ cup.
4 Combine oranges, grapefruit, walnuts and leaves in a large bowl. Thinly slice duck on the diagonal and toss through salad. To serve, divide salad among plates and drizzle dressing over.
Serves 4-6

VARIATIONS

✳ Place ½ cup fresh orange juice, 60ml fino sherry, 2 tbsp walnut oil and ½ tsp ground cumin in a bowl and whisk to combine, add 2 butterflied spatchcock, turn to coat, then cover and refrigerate overnight. Remove spatchcock from marinade and roast at 200C until golden and cooked through. Cut spatchcock into quarters, then serve warm with the orange, pink grapefruit and walnut salad to the side.

✳ Pan-fried duck breasts are excellent with a pear, hazelnut and mâche [lamb's lettuce] salad. Halve and core 3 firm but ripe Bartlett or Anjou pears, then thinly slice lengthways and place in a bowl with ¾ cup hazelnuts, 2 punnets mâche and 100g baby spinach leaves. Make the dressing with hazelnut oil instead of walnut oil, divide salad among plates, top with sliced duck breasts and drizzle over dressing.

✳ Use 4 prepared confit duck legs instead of duck breast fillets. Pan-fry duck confit pieces in an ovenproof frying pan until the skin is crisp, then transfer to a 180C oven until warmed through. Substitute radicchio and endive with 1 large bulb of fennel, trimmed and thinly shaved and 150g picked watercress or mesclun. Rendered duck fat can be refrigerated and used for roasting crisp potatoes.

VERJUICE-POACHED CHICKEN AND BABY LEAVES WITH BASIL SALAD CREAM

750 ml verjuice or dry white wine

2 fresh bay leaves

4 black peppercorns

3 sprigs each of thyme and flat-leaf parsley

3 chicken breast fillets

100 g baby endive leaves

100 g baby rocket leaves

1 baby cos, trimmed, washed, dried and torn into bite-size pieces

2 tbsp extra-virgin olive oil

2 tsp white wine vinegar

1 avocado, halved, seeded, peeled and cut into 1cm-thick slices

BASIL SALAD CREAM

½ cup pouring cream

⅓ cup sour cream

1 tsp Dijon mustard

1 tsp lemon juice, or to taste

¼ cup coarsely chopped basil

1 Place verjuice, bay leaves, peppercorns and herbs in a large, deep frying pan and bring to the boil, then simmer for 5 minutes. Add chicken and simmer over very low heat for 10 minutes or until chicken is just tender. Remove pan from heat and stand, covered, for 15 minutes. Remove chicken with a slotted spoon, discard cooking liquid, then cool slightly and tear into bite-size pieces.

2 Meanwhile, for basil salad cream, combine creams, mustard and lemon juice in a small bowl, season to taste and whisk to combine. Cover closely with plastic wrap and refrigerate until required. Just before serving, stir in chopped basil. Makes about ¾ cup.

3 Place salad leaves in a large shallow bowl or on a large plate, add olive oil and vinegar, season to taste and toss to combine, then top with avocado and chicken. Drizzle with a little basil salad cream and serve immediately with remaining basil salad cream passed separately.

Serves 4 as a light meal

VERJUICE

Derived from the French word 'verjus', which means green juice, verjuice is the uncooked, acidic liquid that results from pressing unripe grapes. Traditionally produced by the winemaking regions of France and Spain, verjuice is an integral ingredient used in their local cuisines. In the UK, where it was a popular ingredient in the Middle Ages, it was once made from crabapples. Its flavour is used to add a subtle sour note to salad dressings, sauces, braises, fish stock and court bouillon. It is also excellent when used in sweet dishes, such as the poaching liquid for fruit or when added to cakes instead of liqueur.

HARISSA AND CORIANDER-MARINATED CHICKEN BROCHETTES WITH ROASTED CAPSICUM AND OLIVE SALAD

HARISSA AND CORIANDER-MARINATED CHICKEN BROCHETTES WITH ROASTED CAPSICUM AND OLIVE SALAD

1 tsp harissa [see Glossary]

¼ cup olive oil

¼ cup chopped coriander

1 kg chicken breast fillets, cut into 2cm pieces

12 bamboo skewers, soaked in water for 30 minutes

ROASTED CAPSICUM AND OLIVE SALAD

2 red capsicum, grilled until skins blacken and blister, peeled, seeded and cut into 1-2cm strips

75 g [½ cup] kalamata olives, pitted

150 g yellow teardrop tomatoes

2 tbsp extra-virgin olive oil

3 tsp aged red wine vinegar

1 Place harissa, olive oil and coriander in a bowl, season to taste and whisk to combine. Place chicken in a ceramic or glass bowl, add harissa mixture and stir to combine, then cover and refrigerate for at least 2 hours or overnight.

2 Thread 5 pieces of chicken onto each bamboo skewer, then char-grill or barbecue on a hot flat plate for 6-8 minutes, turning halfway through cooking or until cooked through.

3 For roasted capsicum and olive salad, combine all ingredients in a shallow bowl and season to taste. Serve brochettes with roasted capsicum and olive salad passed separately.

Serves 4-6

CHARRED CORN, CAPSICUM AND CHICKEN SALAD

2 cups milk

1 tsp dried chilli flakes

3 corn cobs, husks and silk removed

Extra-virgin olive oil

¼ cup red wine vinegar

1 clove of garlic, finely chopped

3 small capsicum [red, yellow and green], finely chopped

1 small Spanish onion, finely chopped

1 cup [loosely packed] basil leaves, torn

¼ cup coarsely chopped flat-leaf parsley

2 chicken breast fillets [about 400g], char-grilled for 2-3 minutes each side, then thinly sliced

1 Place milk and chilli flakes in a large saucepan with 1 litre water, bring to the boil and add corn cobs, adding more boiling water if necessary to cover corn. Cook for 5 minutes or until tender, then remove and drain.

2 Brush corn cobs lightly with oil, then char-grill or barbecue, turning often, for 4-5 minutes or until kernels are golden. Cool slightly, then remove kernels [see page 253].

3 Whisk together ½ cup olive oil and red wine vinegar in a small bowl, then add garlic and season to taste. Place corn, capsicum, onion, basil, parsley and chicken in a large bowl, add dressing, toss gently to combine and serve.

Serves 4 as a light meal

TURKEY AND PEACH SALAD WITH POMEGRANATE AND ORANGE DRESSING

150 g mesclun

100 g wild rocket

2 radicchio, outer leaves discarded

1 kg cooked turkey meat, coarsely chopped

6 freestone peaches or white nectarines, halved, stoned and cut into wedges

Dark rye bread and unsalted butter, to serve

POMEGRANATE AND ORANGE DRESSING

⅓ cup pomegranate molasses [see Glossary]

Juice of 2 large oranges

2 cups olive oil

2 tsp Dijon mustard

1 For dressing, place all ingredients in a screw-top jar, season to taste and shake until well combined, then set aside for 30 minutes for flavours to develop. Makes about 3 cups.

2 Place leaves in the base of a large, shallow serving bowl, scatter with turkey, then peaches, drizzle generously with dressing and toss gently to combine. Serve immediately with dark rye bread and unsalted butter passed separately.

Serves 8

VARIATIONS

✱ The fresh, fruity flavours of this salad also complement the richness of duck meat. Place ¼ cup olive oil, ½ tsp each ground allspice and ground ginger in a bowl and whisk to combine, then brush over 4 duck breast fillets. Heat olive oil in a frying pan, cook duck breasts, skin-side down, until golden, then turn and cook until medium rare. Slice on the diagonal and add to salad, drizzle with pomegranate and orange dressing and serve immediately.

✱ Remaining pomegranate and orange dressing can be used as a marinade for barbecued quail. Place 4 butterflied jumbo quail in a bowl, add dressing, season to taste and turn to coat, then cover and refrigerate for at least 2 hours. Remove quail from marinade, then barbecue over medium high heat until just cooked through. Serve with a salad of quartered black figs, orange segments, watercress sprigs, torn flat-leaf parsley and round mint.

✱ Add sliced poached chicken breast to this salad instead of turkey, along with torn prosciutto and use rocket instead of mesclun. For an Italianate dressing, place 1 tbsp fig vincotto, ⅓ cup extra-virgin olive oil, 1 tsp Dijon mustard and 1 clove of garlic, finely chopped, in a bowl, season to taste and whisk to combine, then add to salad. Or omit the chicken from the salad, and serve salad as a picnic accompaniment to cold roast chicken.

SALAD OF WARM CHICKEN LIVERS, PANCETTA AND BABY ENDIVE

Olive oil

180 g piece of pancetta, cut into 5mm pieces [see Glossary]

1 shallot, finely chopped

55 g [⅓ cup] blanched whole almonds, roasted and halved

450 g chicken livers, cleaned

2 tbsp plain flour

⅓ cup sherry vinegar [see page 15]

1 baby endive, trimmed, washed and torn

1 Heat 1 tbsp olive oil in a non-stick frying pan, add pancetta and cook, stirring frequently, over medium heat for 5 minutes or until golden. Add shallot and stir until soft, then stir in almonds and transfer to a large bowl.

2 In same pan, heat 2 tbsp olive oil. Dust chicken livers in flour, shake away excess, then cook, in 2 batches, until browned but still pink in the middle. Return all livers to pan, add sherry vinegar and cook until bubbling, then spoon into bowl. Add endive and 1½ tbsp olive oil to bowl and season to taste. Toss well, divide among 4 bowls and serve immediately.

Serves 4 as a light meal

CHICKEN LIVERS

To clean chicken livers, rinse under cold running water, then using a small, sharp knife, carefully remove and discard any connective tissue, green or dark spots and fat, and gently pat dry with absorbent paper. For larger livers, separate the two lobes of each liver. Choose the palest chicken livers possible, as darker red ones often taste bitter.

Where possible, choose fresh livers over frozen ones to ensure the highest quality and nutritional value. Chicken livers are an excellent source of iron and vitamin A. Refrigerate loosely wrapped for no more than a day.

WARM ASPARAGUS, CHICKEN AND TOASTED BREAD SALAD WITH WALNUT VINAIGRETTE

2 cups chicken stock

1 clove of garlic, bruised

½ tsp black peppercorns

2 chicken breast fillets [about 200g each]

½ loaf of ciabatta, crust removed, torn into long, bite-size pieces

Extra-virgin olive oil

1 bunch of asparagus, trimmed

350 g peas, podded [about 1 cup podded]

100 g [1 cup] walnuts, roasted

2 witlof, trimmed and leaves separated

WALNUT VINAIGRETTE

1 tsp Dijon mustard

1 tbsp sherry vinegar

1 tbsp walnut oil

2 tbsp olive oil

1 Place stock, garlic, peppercorns and ½ tsp sea salt in a small saucepan and bring to the boil. Add chicken, reduce heat and simmer very gently for 5 minutes, then cover, remove from heat and stand until chicken is just cooked through.

2 Meanwhile, for walnut vinaigrette, place all ingredients in a small bowl, season to taste and whisk to combine well. Makes about ⅓ cup.

3 Place bread on an oven tray, drizzle with olive oil and season to taste, then bake at 200C for 15 minutes or until crisp and golden.

4 Drain chicken, tear into large pieces, then place in a bowl with 2 tbsp dressing and toss to combine well.

5 Cook asparagus and peas, separately, in boiling salted water for 3-4 minutes or until tender, then drain and add to chicken with toasted bread, walnuts and witlof. Drizzle over remaining dressing, divide among 4 bowls and serve immediately.

Serves 4 as a light meal

CROUTONS

✱ To make classic croutons, remove the crust from half a loaf of day-old sourdough bread and cut into 1-2cm pieces. Heat 60g butter in a frying pan until melted and foaming, then add half the bread pieces, stir to coat in melted butter, then cook, stirring frequently, over medium heat for 5 minutes or until crisp and golden and drain on absorbent paper. Repeat with extra butter and remaining bread. For garlic croutons, add a halved clove of garlic to the butter before adding bread, then remove and discard garlic. Croutons can be stored in an airtight container for up to 7 days.

✱ For different flavoured croutons, try using walnut or hazelnut oil instead of olive oil or butter; use different breads such as cornbread, walnut bread or pumpernickel; toss bread in ¼ cup finely grated Parmigiano Reggiano and olive oil, before baking at 180C for 20 minutes; toss bread pieces in olive oil combined with chopped fresh herbs such as thyme, sage or rosemary before baking or pan-frying; or add finely chopped bacon or pancetta to the oil when pan-frying croutons.

PHEASANT, PARSNIP, APPLE AND PANCETTA SALAD WITH BARBERRY DRESSING

2 parsnips [about 160g each]

2 sundowner or pink lady apples

1 kg pheasant

2 tsp olive oil

2 tsp butter

6 thin slices pancetta [about 75g], halved [see Glossary]

1 tsp marjoram leaves

2 tsp lemon thyme leaves

4 cups baby spinach leaves

1 cup baby red chard leaves

1 cup baby sorrel leaves

BARBERRY DRESSING

15 g [¼ cup] barberries, soaked in ½ cup boiling water for 2 minutes, then drained [see Glossary]

¼ cup apple cider vinegar

2 tbsp honey

¼ cup olive oil

Pheasant is only in season from early autumn to mid-winter, but guinea fowl makes a good substitute.

1 Peel parsnips and halve lengthways, then cut into thirds widthways, cutting larger pieces into four lengthways. Core apples and cut into 8 wedges, leaving skin on.

2 Using a heavy sharp knife, prepare pheasant by cutting off feet and wings, leaving first joint attached, and discard, then cut down either side of the backbone and discard bone. Turn pheasant over and flatten breasts, then cut in half on either side of the breastbone and discard breastbone. Rinse pheasant under cold water, pat dry with absorbent paper and season to taste.

3 Heat 1 tsp olive oil in a large heavy-based frying pan, add pheasant pieces, skin-side down, and cook over high heat for 1-2 minutes or until skin is browned. Turn over and cook for another minute, then transfer pheasant to a baking paper-lined ovenproof dish, reserving pan.

4 Heat butter and 1 tsp remaining olive oil in reserved pan, add parsnips and cook over high heat for 2 minutes, add apples and cook for another minute, then season to taste. Scatter apples, parsnips and pancetta around pheasant. Roast at 225C for 10 minutes, then add marjoram and lemon thyme, reduce temperature to 170C and cook for 12-15 minutes or until pheasant and vegetables are tender.

5 Meanwhile, for barberry dressing, combine all ingredients in a bowl and season to taste. Makes about ¾ cup.

6 To serve, cut pheasant legs in half and breasts into 3-4 pieces. Place spinach leaves on plates, top with pheasant, parsnip, apple and pancetta, drizzle dressing over, then scatter with baby chard leaves and sorrel.

Serves 4

seafood

Many seafood lovers consider that their favourites, especially shellfish, are more delicious served in a salad than in any other way. Certainly, a seafood salad is the fastest and easiest way to a stunning summer lunch. And, on a practical note, an escort of interesting vegetables not only sets off the luxurious flavours and texture of seafood, but makes these often expensive delicacies go further. New angles on the subject run from a barbecued squid salad in the Mediterranean manner, to salads that use Australia's excellent farmed Atlantic salmon, or the native Australian freshwater crustacean, marron.

A bonus of many seafood salads is that they allow you to cook the fish or shellfish in the calm period, ahead of last-minute preparations, when you can concentrate on watching carefully and cooking it to perfection. Fish is ready as soon as the flesh is white [or pink, for salmon] and opaque, and when a toothpick will slide in easily. Shellfish is cooked when the flesh is opaque or, if in the shell, when the shell changes colour. If you prefer your scallops rare, cook them only until the outside is white but they still feel bouncy.

seafood varieties

CRABS [1]
The major commercial varieties are blue swimmer and spanner crabs [both small] and mud crabs [large]. They should be heavy for their size and smell fresh. Blue swimmers are sold both raw [but not live] and cooked, spanners are sold cooked. Mud crabs are sold live – place in the freezer for about one hour before cooking.

SCALLOPS [2]
These succulent shellfish are usually sold shelled, though you may find them still in their fan-shaped shells, which make attractive containers for a starter. Scallops are sometimes sold complete with their edible orange roe.

SCAMPI [3]
Scampi are related to both prawns and lobsters – they look rather like very small lobsters, and have similar tails, containing the meat, which are often sold separately. Fresh, unfrozen ones are best but may be hard to find; however, frozen can be satisfactory if thawed slowly and cooked gently and only until the meat is opaque.

RED MULLET [4]
No relation to the grey mullet, but a much smaller, superbly flavoured fish much-prized by Provençal and Italian cooks. Usually sold whole.

BABY OCTOPUS [5]
You can usually buy octopus already cleaned. Babies are usually tender, but if in doubt, freeze them overnight, then thaw, which partially breaks down the tissues and makes the flesh tender.

TIGER PRAWNS, KING PRAWNS [6]
Both varieties can be bought green [raw] or cooked. They can be very large, but medium-size are sweeter and more tender.

GARFISH [7]
Usually sold whole, garfish are moist and delicate in flavour. The large backbone is easily removed, leaving only small, soft bones.

BLACK MUSSELS
The best mussels are alive and as recently harvested as possible, so the wild black Australian mussel or the farmed blue one are preferable to imports. Remember to buy a few more than you need to allow for those that do not open when cooked.

MARRON
These freshwater crayfish are superb delicacies. They are farmed as well as wild-caught and can grow to 1kg in weight. Handle and cook in the same way as rock lobster.

ROCK LOBSTERS
Buy lobsters either alive or cooked – never accept a dead green [raw] lobster, as the flesh spoils rapidly after death. They should be heavy for their size and smell fresh. Immediately before cooking, place live lobster in ice water and stand for about one hour.

SMOKED TROUT
Available at fish markets, good fishmongers and some delicatessens. Usually sold whole. To prepare, peel away the thick outer skin, lift the fillets [two on each side] off the bone, then feel for the fine pin bones and pull them out with tweezers.

SNAPPER
A firm-fleshed, flavoursome white fish that comes in sizes from 500g to 2kg. Available whole and as cutlets.

SQUID, CUTTLEFISH
These close relatives are handled and cooked in the same way. Squid is sold whole, or as cleaned, ready-to-cook bodies [sacs] which can be stuffed or sliced for calamari rings. Cuttlefish, which is more tender than squid, is usually sold whole.

GRILLED SWORDFISH SALAD

3 tsp fennel seeds

3 tsp coriander seeds

1½ tsp white peppercorns

4 baby artichokes or 8 artichokes preserved in oil, halved

½ cup lemon juice

4 swordfish steaks [about 200g each]

2 tbsp olive oil

2 baby cos, leaves separated and washed

2 small bulbs of fennel, trimmed, green fronds reserved, shaved

160 g shaved parmesan

VERJUICE DRESSING

½ cup verjuice [see page 144]

½ cup extra-virgin olive oil

1 Place fennel seeds, coriander seeds and peppercorns in a mortar and, using a pestle, grind to a fine powder.

2 If using fresh artichokes, cut off one-third at the tip and remove the tough outer leaves and green parts from stem. Using a teaspoon or melon baller remove the hairy choke and discard. Thinly slice artichoke and toss in a bowl with ¼ cup lemon juice, then drain off excess juice.

3 Rub spices liberally over swordfish, season to taste with sea salt and drizzle all over with olive oil. Heat a heavy-based frying pan, add fish and cook for 2 minutes, then turn and cook for another minute for medium rare or until cooked to your liking. Transfer fish to a flat container and drizzle with remaining lemon juice. Cool slightly, then break fish into 3-4 pieces and return to container.

4 For verjuice dressing, whisk together verjuice and oil in a bowl and season to taste. Makes about 1 cup.

5 Place cos, fennel, artichokes, parmesan, swordfish and dressing in a large bowl and toss gently to combine. Serve salad divided among plates with swordfish cooking juices poured over and scattered with reserved fennel fronds.

Serves 4-6

MANDOLIN

Mandolins are a hand-operated tool used for slicing firm vegetables such as fennel, carrots, potatoes, celeriac, onions and beetroot into different shapes. The stainless steel or wooden frame holds 2 adjustable blades, one that is plain and the other serrated, which can be alternated depending on whether vegetables are to be grated, cut into julienne or french fries, shaved or waffle cut. It is important to use a hand guard, as the blades are extremely sharp. This traditional French kitchen utensil was used before food processors, and achieves a finer, more uniform result. For more information, see page 278.

BARBECUED SQUID, ENDIVE AND OLIVE SALAD WITH ROMESCO SAUCE

600 g baby squid, cleaned with tentacles reserved, scored and cut into triangles

2 tbsp olive oil

1 tsp sweet Spanish paprika

¼ tsp dried chilli flakes

2 red capsicum, roasted until skins blacken and blister, peeled, seeded and thinly sliced

150 g baby endive [see page 22]

2 vine-ripened tomatoes, cut into wedges

60 g [⅓ cup] Ligurian or other small black olives [see page 241]

6 anchovy fillets

ROMESCO SAUCE

2 large vine-ripened tomatoes

2 fresh long red chillies

¼ tsp sweet Spanish paprika

Extra-virgin olive oil

50 g [⅓ cup] hazelnuts, lightly roasted, peeled

1 red capsicum, roasted until skin blackens and blisters, peeled, seeded and coarsely chopped

3 cloves of garlic, chopped

3 tsp aged red wine vinegar

1 tbsp lemon juice

1 For romesco sauce, place tomatoes, chillies, paprika and 2 tsp oil in a bowl, season to taste and toss to coat well. Cook tomatoes and chillies on a hot char-grill plate, turning frequently, for 4-5 minutes or until soft and skins blister. Cool tomatoes and chillies slightly, then peel, seed and coarsely chop. Process hazelnuts in a food processor until finely ground, then add chopped vegetables, garlic, vinegar and lemon juice and process until a paste forms. With motor running, add ¼ cup oil, then season to taste. Transfer to a bowl, cover closely with plastic wrap and refrigerate until needed. Makes about 1⅔ cups.

2 Place squid, olive oil, paprika and chilli flakes in a bowl, season to taste and toss to combine. Char-grill or barbecue squid, including reserved tentacles, over high heat for 40 seconds on each side [large tentacles will take slightly longer to cook] or until just opaque.

3 Combine capsicum, endive, tomatoes, olives, anchovies and squid in a bowl, season to taste and toss gently to combine.

4 Divide salad among shallow bowls, then drizzle with romesco sauce and serve, with remaining sauce passed separately.

Serves 6 as a light meal

VARIATIONS

✳ For great picnic fare, split small sourdough rolls in half, spread generously with romesco sauce and top with flaked poached Atlantic salmon, baby cos and char-grilled zucchini.

✳ For the Spanish spring dish calcotada, brush trimmed pencil leeks with olive oil and char-grill until tender. Serve with bowls of romesco sauce for dipping.

✳ Add spoonfuls of romesco sauce to bowls of lobster, tomato and saffron broth, or mussels steamed with white wine, and serve with warm crusty bread.

GRILLED RED MULLET WITH RADISH VINAIGRETTE

GRILLED RED MULLET WITH RADISH VINAIGRETTE

4 whole red mullet [about 250g each], cleaned
Olive oil

1 lemon

4 sprigs of French tarragon
Pita bread, to serve, optional

RADISH VINAIGRETTE

1 small clove of garlic, finely chopped

½ tsp Dijon mustard

¼ cup aged white wine vinegar

½ cup olive oil

2 tsp finely chopped French tarragon
Finely grated rind of ½ orange

2 Lebanese cucumbers,
peeled, seeded and thinly sliced

1 bunch of radishes [about 500g],
trimmed and cut into julienne

1 For radish vinaigrette, place all ingredients except cucumbers and radishes in a bowl with a pinch of sugar, season to taste and whisk until well combined. Makes about ¾ cup.

2 Place red mullet on a well-oiled, foil-lined oven tray. Cut lemon in half widthways and cut one half into thin slices. Divide lemon slices and tarragon among fish cavities. Squeeze remaining lemon half over fish, drizzle with 1 tbsp olive oil and season to taste. Bake fish at 190C for 15-18 minutes or until just tender.

3 Stir cucumber and radishes into vinaigrette in serving bowl. Place fish on a large platter and serve immediately with pita bread, if using.
Serves 4 as a light meal

GARFISH AND FENNEL SALAD

2 bulbs of baby fennel, very thinly sliced

1 stalk of celery, strings removed with
a vegetable peeler, finely chopped

1 wedge of preserved lemon, flesh discarded
and peel finely chopped [see Glossary]

1 cup coarsely chopped flat-leaf parsley

18 garfish, butterflied and boned, leaving
tails intact [ask your fishmonger to do this]

170 g [1 cup] coarse polenta

2 tbsp unsalted butter

2 tbsp olive oil

LEMON DRESSING

¼ cup extra-virgin olive oil

2 tbsp lemon juice

1 clove of garlic, finely chopped

1 For lemon dressing, whisk together oil, lemon juice and garlic and season to taste with freshly ground black pepper. Makes about ⅓ cup.

2 Place fennel, celery, preserved lemon and parsley in a large bowl, pour dressing over and toss to combine.

3 Coat garfish on each side with polenta, shaking off excess. Melt enough butter with oil to cover base of a large non-stick frying pan over high heat. Reduce heat to medium and cook garfish, in batches, for 30-60 seconds on each side or until just cooked through, then drain on absorbent paper.

4 Divide fennel mixture among 6 plates, top each with 3 garfish and serve immediately.
Serves 6

MARRON SALAD WITH CAPELLINI, BABY SPINACH, PARSLEY AND LAMB'S LETTUCE

1.5 kg green marron
500 g capellini [angel hair pasta], or other fine long pasta
2 tsp olive oil
200 g baby spinach, picked
1 bunch of flat-leaf parsley, picked
2 punnets lamb's lettuce [mâche], picked
½ cup classic vinaigrette [see page 26]

1 Place marron in the freezer for 1 hour.
2 Bring a large saucepan of water and 1 tbsp cooking salt to the boil over high heat. Add marron, return to the boil and cook for 5 minutes or until marron turns orange, then for another minute. Drain immediately, refresh marron in iced water and drain again.
3 Meanwhile, cook capellini in boiling salted water until al dente. Drain well, cool, then toss with olive oil, season to taste and divide among shallow bowls.
4 Using a sharp, heavy knife, cut marron tail in half lengthways, then remove meat and discard alimentary tract and shells. Remove claws, then crack and remove meat.
5 Place spinach, parsley and lamb's lettuce in a bowl, add vinaigrette and toss gently to combine.
6 Scatter marron claw meat evenly over capellini, then top with salad and marron tail meat and serve immediately.
Serves 4-6

SALAD OF CAULIFLOWER WITH SEARED SCALLOPS

500	g scallops, without roe
200	ml olive oil
600	g small cauliflower florets, trimmed
3	anchovy fillets
2	tsp Dijon mustard
1	large egg yolk
1½	tbsp lemon juice
2	tbsp crème fraîche
45	g [¼ cup] tiny salted capers, well rinsed and drained

1 Place scallops and ¼ cup olive oil in a bowl, toss gently to combine, then leave for 30 minutes.

2 Cook cauliflower in boiling salted water for 4 minutes or until just tender, then drain and refresh under cold running water and drain again. Pat dry with absorbent paper and place in a bowl.

3 Place anchovies and 1 tsp freshly ground black or white pepper on a chopping board, then, using a sharp knife, mash to form a paste. Transfer paste to a bowl, add mustard and egg yolk and whisk to combine. Whisking continuously, gradually add remaining oil, drop by drop at first, then in a thin, steady stream until mixture is thick and emulsified. Whisk in lemon juice, then crème fraîche. Cover closely with plastic wrap and refrigerate until needed. Makes about 1 cup.

4 Heat a large frying pan over high heat and sear drained scallops for 40 seconds on each side. Transfer to a plate in a single layer, then leave to rest. Transfer any pan juices to cauliflower, add anchovy mayonnaise and capers, then toss gently to combine and divide among bowls. Top cauliflower mixture with seared scallops and serve immediately.

Serves 4-6

SALTED CAPERS

Capers are the edible unopened floral buds of a shrub indigenous to the Mediterranean. They can either be dry cured, then packed in sea salt, pickled in wine vinegar or preserved in brine. Salted capers tend to retain a firmer texture and stronger caper taste and need to be rinsed and soaked in water for 10 minutes before using, to soften their salty flavour. Capers in vinegar or brine generally have a softer texture and also have a vinegary flavour, due to being pickled in liquid. They should be rinsed before use. The smaller capers are the buds that grow at the tip of the bush. The smaller the better, and therefore the more expensive.

SALMON AND POTATO SALAD WITH WARM BACON DRESSING

600 g piece of Atlantic salmon,
 skinned and pin-boned [see Glossary]
750 g kipfler potatoes, scrubbed
 ⅓ cup olive oil
 6 centre-cut rashers of bacon [about 200g],
 rind removed, cut into 1cm pieces
 1 large shallot, finely chopped
 2 tbsp red wine vinegar
 1 radicchio, trimmed, washed
 and coarsely chopped

1 Place salmon in a large frying pan, cover with water, then bring to a simmer over medium heat and cook for 1 minute. Remove from heat and stand salmon in water until cooled, then drain and flake into large pieces.
2 Cook potatoes in boiling salted water until tender. Cool, then peel and cut into 1cm-thick slices and place in a bowl.
3 Heat 2 tbsp oil in a large, heavy-based frying pan, add bacon and cook, stirring occasionally, over medium heat for 10 minutes or until lightly browned. Using a slotted spoon, remove bacon and add to potatoes.
4 Heat remaining oil in the same pan and cook shallot over medium heat for 2 minutes or until soft. Increase heat to high, add vinegar and stir until mixture comes to a simmer, season to taste, then pour immediately over potatoes and toss well to combine. Add salmon and radicchio, toss gently to combine and serve immediately.
Serves 6 as a light meal

VERJUICE-POACHED SQUID SALAD

 1 kg squid, cleaned, tentacles reserved
 2 cups verjuice [see page 144]
 ½ bulb of celeriac [about 200g], peeled
 1 radicchio, tough outer leaves
 discarded, leaves separated,
 washed, dried and torn into bite-size pieces
 60 g [⅓ cup] pitted green
 olives, halved lengthways
 ⅓ cup French tarragon leaves
 1 clove of garlic, finely chopped
 1 fresh long red chilli,
 seeded and finely chopped
 2 tbsp extra-virgin olive oil
 1 tbsp lemon juice

1 Using a sharp knife, cut squid into 1.5cm-thick slices. Place verjuice in a large saucepan, bring just to a simmer, add sliced squid and tentacles, then reduce heat to low and cook, without boiling, for 3 minutes or until just tender. Remove squid with a slotted spoon, discarding cooking liquid, then season to taste. Cool.
2 Cut celeriac into julienne and toss in a bowl with radicchio, olives and tarragon.
3 Place garlic, chilli, olive oil and lemon juice in a small bowl and season to taste with sea salt, then whisk to combine. Divide radicchio mixture among plates, top with poached squid and drizzle with dressing. Serve immediately.
Serves 4-6

SALMON AND POTATO SALAD WITH WARM BACON DRESSING

MUSSELS WITH CAPSICUM AND FENNEL SALAD

1.5 kg black mussels, scrubbed and bearded
  Crusty bread and lemon wedges, to serve

CAPSICUM AND FENNEL SALAD

1 red capsicum, quartered and seeded

1 small bulb of fennel,
  cut into 5mm-thick slices

2 shallots, halved

2 tbsp red wine vinegar

1 tbsp extra-virgin olive oil

2 tbsp torn flat-leaf parsley

1 For capsicum and fennel salad, cook capsicum, fennel and shallots in a lightly oiled char-grill over high heat until charred on both sides. Cool slightly then chop vegetables finely. Combine vinegar and extra-virgin olive oil, season to taste and whisk well. Pour dressing over vegetables, add parsley and toss to combine.
2 Place mussels and 100ml water in a large saucepan, bring to the boil, then cover and cook over high heat for 3-4 minutes or until mussels open. Remove mussels from pan, discarding any unopened ones, and set aside. Discard liquid. Remove empty half-shells and discard.
3 Divide remaining mussel half-shells among bowls, spoon salad over and season to taste. Serve with crusty bread and lemon wedges.
Serves 4-6 as a light meal

VARIATIONS

✱ To serve steamed mussels with a fennel, tomato and caper salad, place 1 bulb of thinly sliced fennel, 2 finely chopped vine-ripened tomatoes and 2 tsp rinsed salted capers in a bowl. Heat ¼ cup olive oil, ¼ tsp crushed fennel seeds and 1 clove finely chopped garlic in a frying pan, remove from heat, then add 1 tbsp aged cabernet vinegar and stir to combine. Add dressing to salad, toss to combine, then spoon over steamed mussel halves.

✱ For a mussel, celeriac and potato salad, place shelled cooked mussels in a bowl with 750g thickly sliced steamed pink-fir potatoes and ½ small celeriac cut into julienne. To make a tartare dressing, place ½ cup mayonnaise, 1 tbsp Dijon mustard, 1 finely chopped shallot, 2 finely chopped cornichons and 2 tsp lemon juice in a bowl, season to taste and whisk to combine, then add to salad and stir gently to coat other ingredients.

✱ Spoon this capsicum and fennel salad over freshly shucked Sydney rock oysters or serve with barbecued lobster tails. Combine softened butter with chopped dill, finely chopped garlic and sweet Spanish paprika, roll to form a log, then wrap in plastic wrap and refrigerate for 2 hours. Barbecue or char-grill lobster tails over high heat, then serve immediately, topped with slices of dill butter, with capsicum and fennel salad and roasted chat potatoes to the side.

LOBSTER, CELERY HEART AND WITLOF WITH AVOCADO CREAM

2 cooked lobsters [about 700g each], peeled and cut into 1.5cm-thick slices

1 witlof, leaves separated

1 bunch of celery, outer stalks removed

Crisp flatbread, optional, to serve

AVOCADO CREAM

½ small clove of garlic

1 avocado, halved, seeded, peeled and chopped

½ cup pouring cream

2 tsp lime juice, or to taste

1 For avocado cream, place garlic on a chopping board, sprinkle with a large pinch of sea salt and, using the flat side of a large knife, crush garlic and salt together until a smooth paste forms. Process garlic paste and avocado in a food processor until smooth, then add cream and process until just combined. Transfer avocado cream to a bowl, stir in lime juice, season to taste and combine well. Cover closely with plastic wrap and refrigerate until needed. Makes about 1 cup.

2 Place sliced lobster, witlof and celery in a large serving bowl and serve with avocado cream and crisp flatbread to the side, if using.

Serves 6 as an appetiser

CRAB, CUCUMBER AND AVOCADO CUPS

300 g cooked crabmeat, picked over

1 small Lebanese cucumber, peeled, seeded and finely chopped

1 tbsp crème fraîche

2 tbsp chopped chervil

2 tbsp finely chopped chives

2 tbsp lemon-pressed extra-virgin olive oil

2 tsp lemon juice, or to taste

1 tsp finely grated lemon rind

1 small avocado, peeled, seeded and cut into 1cm pieces

Sprigs of chervil and mini toasts or toasted sourdough baguette, to serve

1 Place crab, cucumber, crème fraîche, herbs, oil, lemon juice and rind in a bowl, season to taste and stir to combine. Add avocado and stir gently to combine.

2 Divide crab mixture between six 180ml cups or ramekins, scatter chervil over and serve immediately with mini toasts or toasted sourdough baguette.

Serves 6 as a starter

LOBSTER, CELERY HEART AND WITLOF WITH AVOCADO CREAM

cured, marinated & pickled

Although salting, drying, pickling and smoking originated as ways to make perishable foods keep longer, these methods are appreciated today for the way they concentrate and transform the flavours of meats, fish and some vegetables. You can buy many excellent cured foods, but it is also surprisingly easy to make your own, usually more subtle, versions at home.

Marinating fresh food, usually raw but sometimes cooked, as in the chicken escabeche in this chapter, also changes the original taste, building it into something more complex. Marinating can change textures, too. Cooks in Pacific and South American cultures have long known that marinating seafood in an acid, such as lemon or lime juice, will transform its texture and colour from raw to 'cooked' while retaining exquisite succulence and freshness.

These intensely flavoured ingredients are a simple starting point for a salad. They are already interesting enough to make the dish exciting, so all that is needed is to surround them with vegetables and fruits, raw or cooked, to play their own refreshing or calm flavour notes against the rich complexity of the main ingredient.

*The focus here is on regional Italian, with a light, simple-to-prepare
salad based on bottarga, a specialty of my region, Sardinia. While
this is a perfect dish for cooks who want to be more adventurous,
it is also a meal that everyone will enjoy, with fennel and lemon
adding freshness, and cannellini beans to give it body.*

Giovanni Pilu

BOTTARGA SALAD

Giovanni Pilu – Pilu at Freshwater, Sydney

200 g [1 cup] dried cannellini beans,
    soaked in cold water overnight and drained
  2 bulbs of baby fennel
  1 celery heart
  ⅓ cup extra-virgin olive oil
  2 tbsp lemon juice
 60 g piece of mullet bottarga [see note below]
  2 tbsp thinly sliced flat-leaf parsley
    Toasted bread, to serve

1 Cook beans in a saucepan of boiling water for 30 minutes or until tender, then drain, cool and place in a bowl.
2 Using a mandolin or very sharp knife, thinly shave fennel and celery. Add to beans.
3 Place olive oil and lemon juice in a small bowl and season to taste. Pour dressing over salad and toss gently to combine. Finely slice the bottarga, place the slices over the salad and scatter with parsley. Serve immediately with toasted bread.
Serves 4 as a starter or light meal

BOTTARGA
Hailing from Sardinia and Sicily, bottarga is the salted, pressed and dried roe of either mullet or tuna. The grey mullet version, known as bottarga di muggine, is more subtle and less salty than that made from tuna roe. Traditionally, bottarga is made by salting and hand-massaging long roe sacks to eliminate any air pockets, then pressing them with stone or marble weights or heavy wooden planks. Finally, the roe is sun-dried for two to three months, before being shaved, grated or thinly sliced and used, in small quantities, to enliven salads such as this, or to top pasta.

CLOCKWISE FROM FRONT: SCALLOP AND SNAPPER TARTARE;
JICAMA REMOULADE; TOMATO AND PINK GRAPEFRUIT SALAD

RAW SUMMER PLATE

SCALLOP AND SNAPPER TARTARE

300 g scallops without roe

300 g snapper fillet, skinned and pin-boned

120 ml lime juice

2½ tbsp extra-virgin olive oil

2 tbsp finely chopped chives

JICAMA REMOULADE

750 g [about 2] jicama [yam bean], peeled and cut into julienne [see Glossary]

1 tbsp finely chopped ginger

½ cup classic mayonnaise [see page 19]

TOMATO AND PINK GRAPEFRUIT SALAD

500 g cherry tomatoes, halved lengthways

3 pink grapefruit [about 1.2kg], peeled and pith removed, segmented

¼ cup extra-virgin olive oil

The success of this dish relies on using the freshest produce. Homemade mayonnaise makes the world of difference to the jicama rémoulade. Alternatively, use a good-quality purchased mayonnaise.

1 For scallop and snapper tartare, cut seafood into 7mm pieces, then combine in a bowl with lime juice, cover tightly and refrigerate for 20 minutes or until flesh is opaque. Drain excess liquid and discard, then stir in olive oil and chives and season to taste.

2 For jicama rémoulade, place all ingredients in a large bowl, season to taste and stir gently to combine.

3 For tomato and pink grapefruit salad, place all ingredients in a bowl, season to taste and stir gently to combine.

4 Pass separate bowls of scallop and snapper tartare, jicama rémoulade and tomato and pink grapefruit salad to serve.

Serves 4-6 as a light meal

SALT- AND SUGAR-CURED DUCK BREAST WITH CARAMELISED PEAR AND WILD ROCKET

4 small duck breasts [about 180g each], excess fat trimmed

75 g [⅓ cup] caster sugar

4 just-ripe corella pears, peeled, cored and cut into wedges

50 g butter

½ Spanish onion, thinly sliced into rings

3 cups [loosely packed] wild rocket leaves

CURING MIXTURE

200 g [1 cup, firmly packed] brown sugar

100 g sea salt flakes

50 g coriander seeds, roasted and lightly crushed

10 sprigs of thyme, cut in half

4 small dried chillies, crushed

PEAR DRESSING

55 g [¼ cup] caster sugar

1 firm corella pear, peeled, cored and chopped into 1.5cm pieces

2 tbsp walnut oil

2 tbsp Champagne vinegar

2 tbsp lemon juice

1 For curing mixture, combine all ingredients in a large bowl. Place duck in a non-reactive container [glass, ceramic or stainless steel], then rub curing mixture all over duck pieces. Cover, and place in the refrigerator for 2 hours, then remove duck from mixture, rinse and pat dry with absorbent paper. Refrigerate in an airtight container until needed.

2 Meanwhile, for pear dressing, combine sugar and 1 cup water in a small saucepan, stir over low heat until sugar dissolves, then bring to the boil, add pear pieces and simmer for 20 minutes or until tender, then drain, reserving cooking liquid. Process pear pieces in a food processor until smooth, then, with motor running, gradually add combined oil, vinegar and lemon juice until dressing is emulsified, adding a little of the reserved cooking liquid if dressing is too thick. Season to taste, then cool to room temperature. Makes about 2 cups.

3 Heat a large heavy-based frying pan over low heat, add duck, skin-side down, and cook for 15-20 minutes, pouring off the fat as it is rendered, or until skin is brown and crisp. Turn and cook for another 2 minutes, then remove from pan and keep warm.

4 Place caster sugar in a non-stick frying pan and cook over medium heat, shaking pan occasionally, until dark golden, but not burnt. Taking care, add pear wedges and butter and toss until pears are well coated in caramel, then cook for another 5 minutes or until pears are tender. Transfer pears to a baking paper-lined tray and cool.

5 Cut each duck breast into 6-8 thin slices. Place sliced duck, caramelised pears, onion and rocket in a bowl, pour over enough dressing to coat, then season to taste and toss to combine well. Divide salad among plates and serve immediately.

Serves 4

MELON, CUCUMBER AND HAM SALAD WITH HAZELNUTS

MELON, CUCUMBER AND HAM SALAD WITH HAZELNUTS

½ honeydew melon [about 800g],
  peeled, seeded and cut into 1cm dice

3 Lebanese cucumbers,
  peeled, halved lengthways,
  seeded and sliced on the diagonal

500 g piece of leg ham, coarsely torn

90 g roasted peeled hazelnuts, halved

1½ tsp wholegrain mustard

1 tsp honey

½ clove of garlic, finely chopped

¼ cup olive oil

1 tbsp aged white wine vinegar

1 tbsp walnut oil or olive oil

1 Place melon, cucumber, ham and hazelnuts in a bowl.
2 Combine remaining ingredients in a separate small bowl, season to taste and whisk until well combined. Pour dressing over salad, toss well and serve.
Serves 6 as a light meal

PRESERVED ARTICHOKES WITH PANCETTA AND GARLIC

8 whole artichokes preserved in oil, drained

250 g thickly sliced flat spicy pancetta,
  cut into 2cm pieces [see Glossary]

2 heads of garlic, cloves separated

2 tbsp olive oil

Crusty bread, to serve

1 Place artichokes in a bowl.
2 Place pancetta, garlic and olive oil in a heavy-based frying pan and cook over low-medium heat for 10-12 minutes or until pancetta is crisp and garlic is soft. Pour pancetta and garlic over artichokes, season to taste with freshly ground black pepper and toss gently to combine. Serve immediately with crusty bread to the side.
Serves 4 as a starter or part of an antipasti selection

CHICKEN ESCABECHE

12 chicken drumsticks [about 1.8kg], french-trimmed [see Glossary]

⅓ cup extra-virgin olive oil

2 Spanish onions, thinly sliced into rings

3 carrots, thinly sliced

1 tsp cumin seeds

1 tsp hot paprika

2 bay leaves

3 dried small red chillies

10 sprigs of thyme

3 strips of orange rind

½ cup sherry vinegar [see page 15]

450 ml medium-dry sherry

100 ml orange juice

6 sprigs of thyme, extra, to serve

Classic mayonnaise [see page 19], optional, green salad and sautéed potatoes, to serve

Meaning 'pickled' in Spanish, escabeche is a spicy Spanish sauce used to marinate poached food, especially poultry such as chicken and turkey and fried food, mostly fish. Traditionally, an acidic ingredient, such as vinegar or lime juice, forms the basis of escabeche, and is usually combined with herbs such as bay leaves, flat-leaf parsley, rosemary or thyme, spices, onions and chillies. This not only adds flavour to the marinated ingredient, but also acts as a preservative. Escabeche should always be served at room temperature. Versions of escabeche followed the Spanish in their travels and are also made in Mexico, throughout South America, Jamaica, where it is called escovitch, and North Africa, where it is known as scabetche.

1 Pat drumsticks dry with absorbent paper. Heat olive oil in a large, non-stick frying pan, add drumsticks and cook, turning regularly, over medium heat for 15 minutes or until just cooked. Reserve frying pan and oil. Place drumsticks in a glass or ceramic dish just large enough to hold them in a single layer and season to taste.

2 Reheat oil in pan, add onions, carrots and cumin and cook for 3 minutes, stirring occasionally, until onions are soft but still holding their shape. Add paprika, bay leaves, chilli, thyme, orange rind, vinegar, sherry and orange juice, bring mixture to a simmer and cook for 8 minutes or until carrots are tender. Pour hot mixture over chicken and cool completely.

3 Serve escabeche at room temperature, scattered with extra thyme sprigs, a spoonful of mayonnaise to the side, if using, and green salad and sautéed potatoes.

Serves 6

FIG, PROSCIUTTO, PEAR AND WITLOF SALAD WITH POMEGRANATE VINAIGRETTE

Janni Kyritsis – chef

3 red sensation pears,
   quartered, cored and placed
   in acidulated water [see note below]

3 small heads each of yellow
   and red witlof, leaves separated

6 figs, quartered

12 slices of prosciutto

POMEGRANATE VINAIGRETTE

1 large pomegranate, seeds removed
   Extra-virgin olive oil

1 For pomegranate vinaigrette, reserve ⅓ cup seeds, then place remaining seeds in a heavy sieve over a bowl and, using a wooden rolling pin, crush seeds to extract as much juice as possible, discarding solids. Combine pomegranate juice with an equal quantity of olive oil.

2 Just before serving, drain pears, then thinly slice lengthways. Layer witlof, figs, prosciutto and pears alternately in a large shallow bowl or individual bowls, scatter with reserved pomegranate seeds and pour vinaigrette over. Season to taste and serve immediately.

Serves 4-6 as a starter or light meal

ACIDULATED WATER

Water acidulated with a small quantity of lemon or lime juice, wine or vinegar is used to soak cut fruit and vegetables to prevent them from browning. Fruit including pears, apples, bananas and banana blossoms, and vegetables such as celeriac, globe and jerusalem artichokes, darken when their cut surfaces are exposed to air. Immersing them in acidulated water for brief periods allows them to absorb the liquid and stops browning. To prepare acidulated water, add ¼ cup lemon or lime juice, 1 tbsp vinegar or 125ml wine to 1 litre water.

SALAD OF SPINACH, CHICKPEAS AND HOME-SALTED COD

2 tbsp sea salt

750 g piece of cod, skinned and pin-boned

100 ml extra-virgin olive oil

1 onion, thinly sliced

2 cloves of garlic, finely chopped

1 fresh red birdseye chilli,
   seeded and finely chopped

¼ tsp smoked Spanish paprika

1 tsp cumin seeds

2 tbsp tomato paste

1½ tbsp red wine vinegar

¼ tsp [loosely packed] saffron threads,
   soaked in 1 cup warm water for 10 minutes

400 g cooked chickpeas [200g dried]

120 g [2 cups] baby spinach leaves
   Lemon wedges, to serve

1 Scatter half the salt over the base of a flat glass or porcelain dish that is just large enough to hold cod, then place fish over salt and scatter with remaining salt. Cover with plastic wrap, then weigh down with cans of food and refrigerate for 24 hours.

2 Heat ¼ cup olive oil in a large heavy-based frying pan, add onion and cook over medium heat for 5 minutes. Add garlic and chilli and stir for 2 minutes or until soft, then add paprika and cumin and stir until fragrant. Add tomato paste, stir for 2 minutes, then add vinegar and saffron with soaking water and bring to the boil. Add chickpeas and cook for 5 minutes or until heated through.

3 Drain cod from liquid, rinse and pat dry with absorbent paper, cut into 3 lengthways, then widthways into 1cm slices. Add to simmering chickpea mixture and cook for 3 minutes or until just cooked through. Remove from heat, cool, then stir in remaining olive oil and spinach leaves. Serve with lemon wedges.

Serves 6 as a light meal

VARIATIONS

✳ For a Portuguese rice and salt cod salad, heat olive oil in a frying pan, add 1 finely chopped onion, 2 cloves of chopped garlic, 8 chopped green onions, 2 finely chopped vine-ripened tomatoes and ¼ tsp chilli flakes and cook for 2-3 minutes. Place shredded salt cod, 2 cups cooked long grain rice, onion mixture, ¼ cup each chopped flat-leaf parsley and coriander and 2 tbsp lemon juice in a bowl and stir to combine.

✳ To use purchased salt cod, or bacalao, place a 750g piece of bacalao in a shallow dish, cover with water, then soak in the refrigerator for up to 3 days, changing the water at least 3 times a day. Brands of salt cod vary in levels of saltiness, so some may only require soaking for 1 day, while others may need up to 3 days. To test, taste a piece of salt cod after 1 day – it should have a pleasant salty taste, but not be overwhelming.

The distinctive cuisine of Latin America and the Caribbean showcases the perfect salad in this spicy ceviche [pronounced sev-eech-ay]. Its interest lies in its freshness and simple preparation, using only the best quality ingredients. It requires little cooking – just 'curing' – and it lends itself to various combinations, thus bringing out the creative side of the passionate cook. If you love the freshness of seafood in Japanese sushi, you will adore this ancient technique with the same quality ingredients. Serve it in a colourful bowl or martini glass on a warm summer day, and enjoy the zippy flavours and succulent texture of a dish that brings the ancient world into modern day.

Victor Pisapia

CUBAN CEVICHE

Victor Pisapia – Cheeky Food Group, Sydney

300 g green bay, school or small king prawns, peeled and cleaned, if necessary

300 g Tasmanian scallops, halved or quartered, depending on size

300 g salmon fillet, skinned, pin-boned and cut into 1cm pieces

1 tomato, chopped

1 mango, peeled, seeded and chopped

¼ Spanish onion, chopped

1 jalapeño chilli, seeded and finely chopped [see Glossary]

1 cup lime juice

150 ml orange juice

½ cup [loosely packed] coriander leaves, coarsely chopped

2 tbsp caster sugar, or to taste

1 large pink grapefruit or orange, peeled, segmented and chopped

Popcorn, seasoned to taste with sea salt, roasted cumin seeds and chilli powder, optional, to serve

1 Bring a large saucepan of water to the boil, turn off heat, add prawns to water and stand for 30 seconds. Drain, refresh immediately in iced water, then drain again.

2 Combine par-cooked prawns, scallops, salmon, tomato, mango, onion and chilli in a large bowl, drizzle with lime and orange juices and toss gently to combine. Using a spoon, press seafood into juices to submerge. Cover and refrigerate for 3 hours.

3 Drain seafood, discarding marinade. Add coriander, sugar and grapefruit or orange, season to taste, then mix gently until combined. Spoon ceviche into small bowls and serve with spiced popcorn, if using, passed separately.

Serves 6-8 as a starter or light meal

CURED SALMON WITH ORANGES, MESCLUN AND BABY BEETROOT LEAVES

175 ml olive oil

1 large shallot, very finely chopped

165 g [¾ cup] granulated sugar

175 g sea salt flakes

2 tsp freshly ground white pepper

1 side Atlantic salmon [about 1.5kg], pin-boned

5 large Valencia oranges, peeled and segmented

200 g mesclun

200 g baby beetroot leaves, picked

1 Place olive oil and shallot in a screw-top jar and shake to combine.
2 Combine sugar, sea salt and white pepper in a bowl. Place a piece of foil twice the length of salmon on a work surface, then place half the sugar mixture in the shape of the fillet in the centre of the foil. Place fish, skin-side down, over sugar mixture, then cover with remaining sugar mixture and fold foil securely to form a parcel. Place fish on a tray and refrigerate for 12-18 hours, but no longer.
3 Remove fish from foil and, using a clean kitchen towel, wipe any remaining sugar mixture from fish. Wrap tightly in plastic wrap and refrigerate until required or for up to 10 days.
4 Using a large sharp knife, cut salmon into wafer-thin slices, slicing at a 45-degree angle away from tail end of fillet, and arrange in a single layer around edge of a large chilled plate.
5 Place orange segments, mesclun and beetroot leaves in a bowl and drizzle over half the olive oil and shallot dressing, then toss gently to combine. Place salad in the centre of the serving plate, then drizzle salmon with remaining dressing and serve immediately.
Serves 10-12 as a starter or light meal

OCEAN TROUT CARPACCIO AND WHITE BEAN SALAD

WITH CELERY SALSA VERDE

✱ Process 1 cup coarsely chopped flat-leaf parsley leaves, 1 coarsely chopped celery heart including leaves, ¼ onion, 2 chopped cloves of garlic, 2 drained anchovy fillets, 2½ tbsp lemon juice and 100ml extra-virgin olive oil in food processor until a coarse paste forms. Season to taste and transfer to a large bowl.

Add two 400g rinsed and drained cans of cannellini beans, 90g [¾ cup] pitted Ligurian or other small black olives and 2 cups watercress sprigs and toss gently to combine. Using a thin sharp knife and working at a 45-degree angle to the fillet, cut an 850g, skinned and pin-boned ocean trout or salmon fillet into very thin, wide

slices, dividing slices among plates to cover as you go. Divide white bean salad among plates, drizzle ocean trout with a little extra-virgin olive oil, season to taste and serve immediately.
Serves 6-8 as a starter or light meal

SALAD OF RADISHES AND THEIR GREENS WITH SMOKED TROUT AND STEAMED POTATOES

2 bunches of radishes [about 500g each]

20 g butter

2 tbsp caster sugar

¼ cup lemon-pressed extra-virgin olive oil

1 onion, finely chopped

650 g kipfler potatoes, scrubbed, boiled until tender, cooled, then cut into 3cm slices on the diagonal

2 smoked trout [about 300g each], skin and bones removed and flesh flaked into large chunks

1½ tbsp red wine vinegar

1 Cut tops from radishes, wash well and reserve, then cut radishes in half lengthways and place in a small frying pan just large enough to hold them in a single layer. Add butter, sugar and enough water to come halfway up sides of radishes, then cover with a round of baking paper with a hole cut out of the centre. Cook radishes over medium heat for 10-15 minutes or until tender, then remove paper and boil rapidly, shaking pan occasionally, until liquid is very reduced and radishes are glazed.

2 Heat 2 tbsp lemon oil in a frying pan, add onion and 1 tsp sea salt and cook over medium heat for 8 minutes or until soft. Add potatoes and toss for 5 minutes or until heated through. Add radish tops and cook, covered, for another 5 minutes or until wilted, then transfer mixture to a bowl. Add smoked trout and glazed radishes, drizzle with remaining lemon oil and vinegar, then season to taste and toss gently to combine. Serve immediately or at room temperature.

Serves 4-6

vegetables

If you want to be famous for your vegetable salads, forget the everything-I-found-in-the-refrigerator approach and concentrate on two or three of the most beautiful vegetables of the season, or even just one kind, and celebrate your chosen stars with brilliant dressings, salsas and a supporting cast of delicious garnishes.

For salads like these, the vegetables are often cooked first, then cooled, and the salad served just warm or at room temperature. Check the vegetables frequently while they're cooking and take them off the heat when they are just cooked, not overcooked.

Look in this chapter for accompaniments to add presence, both summer and winter, to simple meats, poultry and seafood. The warm salad of root vegetables, for example, would be superb with corned beef, while the mushroom salad could lift a steak to epicurean heights, and the potato, artichoke and lemon salad would be perfect with hot or cold roast chicken. And, naturally, they would all make rich and interesting contributions to a vegetarian table.

vegetable varieties

BABY FENNEL [1]

An aniseed-flavoured, bulbous vegetable whose crisp, tightly-packed layers can be sliced and eaten raw, or cooked either whole or cut into segments or slices. The feathery tops can be used as a herb. Baby fennel is more delicate in texture and flavour than the larger kind.

TRUSS CHERRY TOMATOES [2]

True vine-ripened tomatoes have great flavour, but there are many impostors – you have to trust your greengrocer. Truss tomatoes (those still attached to the vine) look convincing, but feel them and buy only if they are slightly soft. Oxhearts don't look thrilling, being pink rather than red and often misshapen, but they are juicy, flavoursome treasures. Yellow teardrop tomatoes are delicately sweet and sharp.

ARTICHOKES [3]

These are the buds of a member of the thistle family. Full-size globe artichokes may be boiled or braised to soften the tender flesh at the base of each leaf and the prized heart. Baby artichokes may be cooked or, if very young and tender, eaten raw in a salad.

BELLA ROSSO PEPPERS [4]

A miniature sweet red capsicum, whose round, squat shape is ideal for stuffing and serving for antipasto.

BEETROOT [5, 6]

Full-size or baby red beetroot [6] and the newer golden variety [5] can all be cooked by either boiling or baking, or can be grated and eaten raw. Unlike most vegetables, beetroot can be cooked ahead and reheated without developing a tired flavour.

BABY TURNIP [7]

Small, young turnips have a delicate, slightly sweet taste. They should be firm and have unblemished skins. Their green leaves should be brightly coloured.

CHILLIES [8]

Fresh chillies are green when unripe and red, yellow, brown, purple or almost black when ripe. They contribute flavour as well as heat – green ones have green-capsicum characters while ripe ones are more full-bodied and sweet. Dried chillies have sweet, caramel and smoky flavour notes. Fresh chillies are seldom sold by name in this country, and the greengrocer's description as 'mild' or 'hot' is not always reliable, so you have to make your own judgment, or stick to dried ones from a good spice shop. Generally, the smaller the chilli, the hotter.

ROMAN BEANS [9]

When young, these flat green beans may be cooked like other fresh beans. The bulgier ones are older, with larger and tougher seeds, and are best braised.

ZUCCHINI FLOWERS [10]

The larger male flowers are the ones usually available. The female flowers come with the juvenile fruit still attached. They are most often served whole, stuffed and crumbed or coated in a light batter and deep-fried. They can also be sliced and eaten raw or lightly cooked.

LEBANESE EGGPLANT [11]

Small [15-23cm long], slim, purple eggplant, good for serving whole as individual portions. Sometimes sold as Japanese eggplant.

BABY CAULIFLOWER

Usually cooked whole to make the most of its miniature charm. Drop into plenty of salted boiling water in a non-aluminium saucepan and cook for 6-8 minutes or until just tender.

BROCCOLINI

A hybrid of regular broccoli and Chinese cabbage-family vegetables, with smooth shiny stems and small broccoli-like heads. Stems as well as heads are eaten.

SHIITAKE AND OYSTER MUSHROOMS

Japanese mushrooms that are now cultivated in Australia. Shiitake are meaty-tasting and luxuriously soft in texture; use the caps only as the stems are tough [though they are good for flavouring stock]. Oyster mushrooms, also called shimeji, are mild-flavoured, with a firm but tender texture, best eaten raw or very briefly cooked.

TOMATO SALAD WITH TOMATO DRESSING

TOMATO SALAD WITH TOMATO DRESSING

500 g cherry tomatoes, halved

200 g semi-dried tomatoes

1 tsp caster sugar

2½ tbsp aged red wine vinegar, or to taste

⅓ cup extra-virgin olive oil

TOMATO DRESSING

¼ cup olive oil

100 g whole blanched almonds

4 large cloves of garlic, unpeeled

2 egg tomatoes

1 tbsp sherry vinegar [see page 15]

1 For tomato dressing, heat olive oil in a small frying pan until hot, add almonds and stir for 1-2 minutes or until deep golden, then drain almonds through a fine sieve over a bowl. Reserve oil and drain almonds on absorbent paper. Place garlic and tomatoes in a small ovenproof dish and roast at 190C for 30 minutes or until garlic is soft. Squeeze soft garlic into a food processor, then peel tomato, halve and scoop out seeds and add to garlic with reserved oil and vinegar. Process mixture until smooth and season to taste. Makes about ⅔ cup.

2 Place remaining ingredients, except almonds, in a bowl, season to taste and toss to combine well. Spoon salad onto a large platter and serve with almonds and tomato dressing passed separately.

Serves 8-10 as an accompaniment

BARBECUED TOMATO, CORN AND LIME SALAD

2 limes

4 corn cobs in their husks, soaked in cold water for 10 minutes, then drained

300 g grape or cherry tomatoes

300 g yellow teardrop tomatoes

Olive oil

1 Cut rind and pith from limes, then cut into slices, chop finely and place in a bowl.

2 Char-grill or barbecue corn cobs, turning frequently, for 15 minutes or until tender. Cool slightly, remove husks and silks, then remove kernels so they stay intact in large pieces [see page 253].

3 Toss tomatoes with 1½ tbsp olive oil and char-grill, turning, for 1-2 minutes or until skins char and burst, then combine with corn and lime. Add 2 tbsp olive oil, season to taste and stir gently to combine.

Serves 4-6 as an accompaniment

WARM CUMIN-BRUSHED EGGPLANT AND ZUCCHINI SALAD WITH CURRANT AND PINENUT DRESSING

1½ tbsp ground cumin

½ cup olive oil

6 Lebanese eggplant, thinly sliced lengthways [see Glossary]

6 zucchini, thinly sliced lengthways

80 g soft marinated cow's milk feta

CURRANT AND PINENUT DRESSING

2 tbsp sherry vinegar (see page 15)

2 tsp Dijon mustard

1 clove of garlic, finely chopped

¼ cup extra-virgin olive oil

¼ cup pinenuts, roasted

¼ cup currants, soaked in 2 tbsp dry sherry for 10 minutes

1 For currant and pinenut dressing, combine vinegar, mustard and garlic in a small bowl, then add oil and whisk to combine well. Season to taste, then add pinenuts and currants with their soaking liquid and stir to combine. Makes about ⅔ cup.

2 Combine cumin and olive oil in a small bowl and season to taste. Brush eggplant and zucchini slices with cumin mixture, then barbecue on a grill plate, in batches, over high heat for 2 minutes on each side or until just tender and browned. Place eggplant and zucchini in a large dish, scatter with feta, drizzle with currant and pinenut dressing and serve immediately.

Serve 6-8 as an accompaniment

VARIATIONS

* Dust slices of haloumi or kefalotiri with plain flour, season to taste with ground cumin, then barbecue with the eggplant and zucchini. Place barbecued cheese and vegetables on a large plate, scatter with picked watercress and flat-leaf parsley leaves and drizzle with currant and pinenut dressing, then serve immediately with warmed flatbread and a bowl of kalamata olives passed separately.

* Cut eggplant and zucchini into 2cm pieces, place on soaked bamboo skewers with separated truss cherry tomatoes and red capsicum pieces, brush with cumin oil, then barbecue for 3-4 minutes. Meanwhile, place 1 cup couscous, 2 tsp grated lemon rind, ⅓ cup each coarsely chopped mint and coriander, and currant and pinenut dressing in a bowl, season to taste and stir to combine. Serve skewers with couscous salad.

* The currant and pinenut dressing is also delicious with roasted root vegetables. Place pieces of white and orange sweet potato, scrubbed baby beetroot and baby carrots on a baking tray, drizzle with cumin oil and roast at 200C until tender. Add a little finely chopped preserved lemon rind to dressing, then drizzle over roast vegetables and serve as an accompaniment to barbecued lamb.

POTATO, ARTICHOKE, LEMON AND ROAST ALMOND SALAD

1 thin-skinned lemon [such as meyer – see page 262], scrubbed

4 globe artichokes

750 g kipfler potatoes, scrubbed

100 g whole blanched almonds, roasted

2 tbsp thyme leaves

LEMON DRESSING

3 tsp honey

Juice of 1 lemon, or to taste

½ cup extra-virgin olive oil

1 For lemon dressing, combine all ingredients and season to taste.
2 Slice lemon as thinly as possible, remove seeds, then place slices on a tray in single layer and sprinkle with 1 tbsp sea salt. Stand for 30 minutes, then rinse well, drain and pat dry on absorbent paper.
3 Meanwhile, using a small sharp knife, trim tough outer leaves from artichokes, cut tops from remaining leaves and trim stems to 2cm. Cut artichokes in half lengthways and remove hairy choke, then place in acidulated water (see page 189). Cook artichokes in boiling salted water for 15-20 minutes or until tender. Drain well, then cut in half lengthways.
4 Steam potatoes in a steamer until tender, then, when cool enough to handle, peel and slice in half lengthways. Place warm potatoes in a large bowl, add half the dressing and toss well to combine. Add lemon slices, artichokes, almonds, thyme and remaining dressing, season to taste, then combine well and serve.
Serves 4-6 as an accompaniment

ARTICHOKES

When choosing globe artichokes, look for those with a vibrant colour and tightly closed tops, as artichokes with leaves starting to open are over-mature. As with many vegetables, choose those that feel heavy for their size. A teaspoon or melon baller can easily remove the hairy choke. The bases are usually trimmed as the outer portion of more mature artichokes can be woody and tough, so are best discarded. Trimming the bases also ensures that the artichokes can stand upright during cooking, which is especially important when cooking whole stuffed artichokes.

GREEN BEAN AND WALNUT SALAD WITH VERJUICE VINAIGRETTE

300 g baby green beans, trimmed, blanched and refreshed in iced water

150 g Roman beans, trimmed, blanched, refreshed in iced water and halved

60 g walnut halves, roasted

3 baby cos hearts, cut into wedges

¼ cup coarsely chopped chives

6 hard-boiled eggs, halved

VERJUICE VINAIGRETTE

¼ cup verjuice [see page 144]

¼ cup walnut oil

2 tsp Dijon mustard

1 For verjuice vinaigrette, whisk together verjuice, walnut oil and mustard, then season to taste.
2 Place remaining ingredients in a bowl and combine well, then add dressing, toss to coat and serve immediately.
Serves 4

ALL-GREEN SALAD

200 g podded peas [about 400g unpodded]

400 g [4 cups] sugar snap peas, trimmed

100 g [2 cups] snow pea sprouts

1 Lebanese cucumber, cut into 1cm pieces

4 stalks of celery, cut into 1cm-thick slices

1 cup [firmly packed] flat-leaf parsley, coarsely chopped

½ cup [firmly packed] mint, coarsely chopped

½ cup finely chopped chives

AVOCADO DRESSING

1 ripe avocado, chopped

¼ cup lemon juice

2 tbsp classic mayonnaise [see page 19]

1 For avocado dressing, place all ingredients in a food processor, process until smooth, then season to taste. Makes about ¾ cup.
2 Cook peas in boiling salted water for 2 minutes, then add sugar snap peas and cook for another 2 minutes or until just tender. Drain, refresh in iced water, then drain again.
3 Combine remaining ingredients in a bowl with peas and sugar snap peas, add avocado dressing, combine all ingredients well and serve immediately.
Serves 8 as an accompaniment

GREEN BEAN AND WALNUT SALAD WITH VERJUICE VINAIGRETTE

WARM SALAD OF ROOT VEGETABLES WITH HORSERADISH DRESSING

2 bunches of baby beetroot,
  trimmed and scrubbed

6 small pontiac potatoes
  [about 420g], scrubbed and halved

1 bunch of baby turnips, trimmed
  and peeled, or 2 medium turnips,
  trimmed, peeled and cut into 1cm slices

1 bunch of baby carrots, trimmed and peeled

12 small shallots

1 bulb of garlic, cloves separated

  Olive oil

  Crusty bread, optional, to serve

HORSERADISH DRESSING

1 clove of garlic, finely chopped

1 tbsp horseradish cream

1 tsp wholegrain mustard

2 tsp aged red wine vinegar

2 tsp lemon-pressed extra-virgin olive oil

¼ cup extra-virgin olive oil

1 For horseradish dressing, combine garlic, horseradish and mustard in a bowl, then gradually whisk in vinegar and oils until well combined and season to taste. Makes about ½ cup.

2 Wrap beetroot together in a piece of foil. Place remaining vegetables in a roasting pan, drizzle with olive oil, season to taste and toss to combine, then place wrapped beetroot to one side in pan and roast vegetables at 190C for 1 hour or until tender.

3 Cool vegetables slightly, then peel beetroot and shallots. Cut beetroot in half and divide among bowls with remaining vegetables, drizzle with dressing and serve salad warm with crusty bread, if using.

Serves 4 as a starter or accompaniment

CAULIFLOWER SALAD WITH SALSA BIANCA

6 anchovy fillets, chopped

3 cloves of garlic, chopped

75 g pinenuts, roasted

2 tbsp white wine vinegar

⅓ cup extra-virgin olive oil

600 g cauliflower [about ½ head], cut into florets

¼ cup coarsely chopped flat-leaf parsley

50 g Ligurian olives or other small black olives [see page 241]

1 Process anchovies, garlic and all but 1 tbsp pinenuts in a food processor until finely chopped. With the motor running, gradually add vinegar and oil and process until incorporated, then season to taste.
2 Cook cauliflower in boiling salted water until just tender, then drain, transfer to a bowl and, while still warm, toss with dressing and parsley. Spoon salad into a bowl, scatter with olives and remaining pinenuts and serve warm or at room temperature.
Serves 6 as an accompaniment or part of an antipasti selection

FENNEL AND CELERY SALAD

600 g fennel [about 2 small bulbs], trimmed, halved lengthways and thinly sliced

3 stalks of celery, trimmed and thinly sliced on the diagonal

1 Spanish onion, halved and thinly sliced

¾ cup coriander leaves

¼ cup extra-virgin olive oil

¼ cup red wine vinegar, or to taste

1 Place fennel, celery, onion and coriander in a large bowl and toss together. Season to taste, drizzle with olive oil and vinegar and toss to combine.
Serves 4-6 as an accompaniment or part of an antipasti selection

CAULIFLOWER SALAD WITH SALSA BIANCA

WARM MIXED MUSHROOM, PROVOLONE AND CROUTON SALAD

WARM MIXED MUSHROOM, PROVOLONE AND CROUTON SALAD

200 g swiss brown mushrooms [see Glossary]
200 g button mushrooms
100 g shiitake mushrooms [see Glossary]
150 g oyster mushrooms [see Glossary]
Olive oil
2 shallots, thinly sliced
2 tbsp thyme leaves
2 tbsp chopped chives
2 tbsp balsamic vinegar
10 radicchio leaves, torn
2 cups coarsely chopped baby endive
35 g [⅓ cup] shaved provolone
50 g [½ cup] walnut halves, roasted
1½ tbsp extra-virgin olive oil

OLIVE BREAD CROUTONS

200 g olive bread, crusts
removed and cut into 2cm pieces
2 tbsp extra-virgin olive oil

1 For olive bread croutons, place bread in a small roasting pan, drizzle with olive oil and bake at 200C for 10-15 minutes or until bread is golden and crisp.
2 Wipe mushrooms clean with a damp cloth and cut large ones in half. Heat ⅓ cup olive oil in a large frying pan or wok, add shallots and cook over medium heat for 2 minutes, then add all the mushrooms and cook over medium-high heat for 2-3 minutes or until they begin to soften. Add herbs and balsamic vinegar, season to taste and stir to combine.
3 Place radicchio and endive in a large bowl, add mushroom mixture, shaved provolone, walnuts and olive bread croutons, then drizzle with extra-virgin olive oil and toss well. Serve immediately.
Serves 6 as a light meal

ROASTED CARROT, CAPER AND MINT SALAD

2.2 kg carrots, peeled, halved
widthways, then cut into wedges
⅓ cup extra-virgin olive oil
2½ tbsp balsamic vinegar, or to taste
45 g [¼ cup] capers, drained
¼ cup torn mint leaves

1 Toss carrots with olive oil, then roast, in batches if necessary, in a large roasting pan at 200C, turning occasionally, for 20 minutes or until golden.
2 Place carrots with remaining ingredients in a large bowl, season to taste, then toss gently to combine. Serve salad warm or at room temperature.
Serves 4-6 as an accompaniment or part of an antipasti selection

ROASTED BEETROOT, CAPSICUM AND RADICCHIO SALAD WITH BASIL VINAIGRETTE

4 small beetroot [about 70g each], trimmed

1 tbsp extra-virgin olive oil

1 large red capsicum, grilled until skin blackens and blisters, then peeled, seeded and cut into 2cm pieces

2 small radicchio, outer leaves discarded, leaves torn into bite-size pieces

Baby basil leaves, to serve

BASIL VINAIGRETTE

1½ cups [firmly packed] basil

¼ cup lemon juice

½ cup extra-virgin olive oil

1 Place beetroot in an ovenproof dish, drizzle with olive oil and season to taste, then bake at 200C for 1½ hours or until tender. Cool, then peel and cut into small wedges.

2 Meanwhile, for basil vinaigrette, process basil and lemon juice in a food processor until finely chopped, then with motor running, gradually add olive oil in a thin, steady stream and process until well combined. Season to taste. Makes about 1 cup.

3 Place beetroot, roasted capsicum and radicchio in a bowl, add basil vinaigrette and combine well. Scatter with baby basil leaves.

Serves 6-8 as an accompaniment

SAFFRON-BRAISED LEEKS WITH PRAWN MAYONNAISE

6 medium leeks [about 1.8kg]

600 ml hot vegetable or chicken stock, approximately

Pinch of saffron threads

2 dried bay leaves

¼ cup extra-virgin olive oil

300 g cleaned, chopped cooked prawns

½ cup classic mayonnaise, approximately [see page 19]

Watercress sprigs, to serve

1 Trim green tops and bases of leeks, then cut in half lengthways and wash well between layers. Place leeks in a single layer in an ovenproof dish, cover with hot stock, adding a little more stock, white wine or water if necessary, so leeks are just covered. Add saffron, bay leaves and olive oil, then cover dish tightly with foil and cook at 180C for 40 minutes or until tender. Cool to room temperature.

2 For prawn mayonnaise, combine chopped prawns with enough mayonnaise to just bind, adding a little of the leek braising liquid to thin, if necessary. Scatter with watercress and serve with saffron-braised leeks.

Serves 6 as a starter

ROASTED BEETROOT, CAPSICUM AND RADICCHIO SALAD WITH BASIL VINAIGRETTE

SWEET-POTATO SALAD WITH OLIVE VINAIGRETTE AND CAPERS

SWEET-POTATO SALAD WITH OLIVE VINAIGRETTE AND CAPERS

1.5 kg orange sweet potatoes, peeled, halved
lengthways and cut into 2-3cm pieces

½ cup olive oil

2 tbsp drained small capers,
patted dry with absorbent paper

1 large Spanish onion, halved and thinly sliced

2 tsp brown sugar

½ cup sherry vinegar [see page 15]

55 g [⅓ cup] pitted kalamata olives,
coarsely chopped

⅓ cup coarsely chopped flat-leaf parsley

10 slices of prosciutto, cooked under
a hot grill until crisp, then coarsely broken

1 Steam sweet potato in a steamer until just tender, then transfer to a bowl and cool.
2 Heat 1 tbsp olive oil in a small frying pan, add capers and stir for 1-2 minutes or until crisp, then using a slotted spoon remove from pan. Add onion, brown sugar and a little more olive oil if necessary to same pan and stir for 8 minutes or until onion is soft and slightly caramelised, then add sherry vinegar and remove from heat.
3 Combine onion mixture, remaining olive oil, olives, parsley and crisp prosciutto, then season to taste and mix well. Pour dressing over sweet potato in bowl and toss gently to combine. Serve scattered with crisp capers.
Serves 6-8 as an accompaniment

ROASTED PUMPKIN, APPLE AND CHESTNUT SALAD

450 g jap pumpkin, peeled,
seeded and thinly sliced

2 pacific rose or royal gala apples,
halved, cored and cut into wedges

2 tbsp extra-virgin olive oil,
plus extra, for drizzling

1 tbsp balsamic vinegar,
plus extra, for drizzling

200 g [1 cup] whole cooked,
peeled chestnuts [see Glossary]

1 cup rocket leaves

2 cups watercress sprigs

1 Cut pumpkin slices in half widthways and combine with apple, olive oil and balsamic vinegar in a large oiled roasting pan, then roast at 180C for 20 minutes or until tender.
2 Add chestnuts and roast for another 5 minutes or until chestnuts are heated through, then stand mixture for 10 minutes until cooled slightly.
3 Combine rocket and watercress in a large bowl, add roasted pumpkin mixture, season to taste and toss well. Divide salad among 4 bowls, drizzle with a little extra olive oil and balsamic vinegar to taste and serve immediately.
Serves 4 as an accompaniment

cheese & eggs

Today's cheese and egg salads are a far cry from those your mother made – a jumble of chilly vegetables with hard-boiled eggs and/or any old cheese somewhere in the crowd. The aim now is to celebrate two of the world's most glorious foods by surrounding them with just the right companions to bring out their charms, and by presenting them at just the right temperature – room-temperature to warm for cheese, just-warm to hot for eggs.

A salad like this can play any number of roles in your life. The more substantial ones add up to a comfortable little meal for those times when you want something easy to eat that's satisfying but not heavy. Several in this chapter would be perfect for a light meal before or after a night out, or when you're eating alone, or for a quiet lunch with a friend. They would also make elegant first courses for more serious lunches or dinners. The lighter salads are designed as accompaniments of distinction. The celery heart and olive salad would make an impression with cold roast beef or ham; the witlof, walnut and parsley with chicken; and the char-grilled pumpkin with roast lamb or chops.

cheese & egg varieties

HENS' EGGS [1], PULLET EGGS [9]
The best eggs have richly coloured yolks and thick whites and are full-flavoured. Always buy free-range, and store in the refrigerator. Pullet eggs, from young hens just starting to lay, are half to three-quarters the size of hens' eggs.

STILTON [2]
One of the three great blue cheeses [the others are roquefort and gorgonzola] made in the English Midlands. Softish, pungent, marvellous with port and walnuts or fresh pear and a fine Australian sticky wine.

PECORINO [3], PECORINO PEPATO
A hard, pungent Italian cheese, originally made from sheep's milk but now also from cow's milk. It is also made in Australia. Used for grating, but also an excellent table cheese, which tends to crumble slightly when cut. Pecorino pepato is studded with peppercorns.

ASIAGO [4]
A firm, salty, tangy Italian cheese.

MOZZARELLA [5]
A waxy, nutty-tasting Italian cheese, now also made in Australia. Classically made from buffalo milk [as some, both Italian and Australian, still is, when it is called mozzarella bufala], but now also made from cow's milk. Melts readily, much used for pizza. Cherry-size balls of soft, white, freshly made mozzarella are called bocconcini.

FRESH GOAT'S CHEESE [6]
Soft, moist, white curd with a delicate creamy flavour. Best eaten the day you buy it; keeps, refrigerated, only a day or two.

GOAT'S CHEESE LOG [7, 8]
Mature goat's cheese [chèvre affiné] has the most developed flavour. It is available in a small log shape, ideal for slicing.

QUAIL EGGS [10]
These little eggs are prized for their decorative effect in a dish. They taste like hens' eggs and are often used hard-boiled, which takes about 4 minutes from placing them [at room temperature] in lightly salted simmering water. Four minutes gives just-set yolks; add a minute or two for really firm ones. Quail eggs have very hard shells — to peel hard-boiled ones, place in iced water for 3 minutes first, tap all over to break the shell and peel from the rounded end.

FETA
A sheep or goat's cheese cured in brine, made in Greece, Turkey and the Balkans and also in Australia. Salty/sharp in flavour, it can be firm or soft. Because of its high moisture content, it does not keep well but soft feta is often marinated, with herbs and other flavourings, in olive oil and will keep for a long time.

HALOUMI
A rubbery, salty, white cheese, originally from Cyprus but now also made in Australia. Haloumi is virtually always served sliced and gently fried in olive oil to brown the outside, which makes it taste deliciously savoury.

MILAWA BLUE
One of Australia's best blue cheeses, with a firm creamy body and big flavour.

PARMESAN
The king of Italian hard cheeses [now also made in Australia]. Often used for grating over pasta, but also a splendid table cheese. The best is Parmigiano Reggiano from the strictly defined Emilia-Romagna cheese-making region in northern Italy. Buy parmesan by the piece, never ready-grated.

WARM SPINACH-WRAPPED SOFT GOAT'S CHEESE WITH RED SALAD

1 bunch of spinach [about 325g], trimmed and washed

2 150g rounds of fresh goat's cheese
   Extra-virgin olive oil, for drizzling

4 fresh bay leaves

2 tsp thyme leaves
   Grissini or sourdough bread, to serve

RED SALAD

⅓ cup olive oil

1½ tbsp red wine vinegar
   Few drops of walnut oil, optional

1½ tsp honey

1 tsp wholegrain mustard

2 trimmed large beetroot [about 840g]

½ Spanish onion, halved and thinly sliced

1 radicchio, outer leaves discarded, thinly shredded

2 red witlof, bases trimmed and thinly sliced lengthways

1 For red salad, whisk together olive oil, red wine vinegar, walnut oil, if using, honey and mustard and season to taste. Place unpeeled beetroot in a small saucepan, cover with water and bring to the boil. Simmer beetroot over medium heat for 50-60 minutes or until tender, then drain. Cool and peel, then cut into julienne or grate and place in a bowl. Combine onion and 1 tsp salt in a sieve over a bowl and stand for 30 minutes, then rinse with water, drain and pat dry. Combine beetroot, softened onion and remaining ingredients in a bowl, add dressing and toss gently to combine.

2 Pick 15-20 large leaves from spinach [reserve remaining leaves for another use]. Place spinach leaves in a bowl and cover with boiling water, drain immediately, then refresh in iced water and drain again. Spread out leaves on absorbent paper, then pat dry with more absorbent paper. Cut each goat's cheese round in half widthways. Place 3-4 spinach leaves [enough to cover cheese] on a work surface, place a round of cheese in the middle, drizzle with olive oil, add a bay leaf and sprinkle with thyme and cracked black pepper. Fold spinach over to enclose cheese, then gently rub parcels with a little more olive oil.

3 Heat a heavy-based frying pan or char-grill until very hot, add parcels and cook for 2-3 minutes each side or until slightly charred. Serve warm spinach-wrapped goat's cheese on a bed of red salad with grissini or sourdough bread.

Serves 4 as a starter or light meal

STILTON, BEETROOT AND SMOKED DUCK SALAD

1 bunch of watercress, sprigs picked

1 bunch of baby golden or
   red beetroot, boiled in salted water
   until tender, cooled, peeled and quartered

2 firm corella pears, halved,
   cored and thinly sliced lengthways

2 smoked duck or chicken breasts,
   half trimmed of fat and thinly sliced

170 g Stilton, crumbled

CHAMPAGNE VINAIGRETTE

⅓ cup walnut oil

2 tsp Champagne vinegar

½ tsp Dijon mustard

¼ tsp lemon juice

1 For Champagne vinaigrette, whisk together all ingredients in a small bowl until well combined, then set aside. Makes about ⅓ cup.
2 To serve, place watercress, beetroot, pears, duck and Stilton in a large bowl, pour dressing over, season to taste and toss gently to combine.
Serves 4 as a starter or light meal

DUCK BREAST
To replace smoked duck breast with cooked fresh duck breast, trim excess fat from a duck breast fillet with the skin on. Score skin and season to taste with sea salt and freshly ground black pepper, then heat 1 tsp olive oil in a large, heavy-based frying pan and cook duck breast, skin-side down, over medium heat for 8-10 minutes or until skin is golden. Turn duck breast over and cook for another 6-8 minutes, then remove from heat and leave, covered with foil, for 10 minutes. Thinly slice duck on the diagonal, then serve with the Stilton and beetroot salad.

CHAR-GRILLED PUMPKIN SALAD WITH PRESERVED LEMON AND OLIVE DRESSING

CHAR-GRILLED PUMPKIN SALAD WITH PRESERVED LEMON AND OLIVE DRESSING

1 jap pumpkin [about 1 kg], cut
  into 4 cm wedges, seeds removed
100 ml olive oil
⅓ cup thinly sliced preserved
  lemon [see Glossary]
250 g dried black olives or
  kalamata olives, pitted
200 g goat's milk feta,
  chopped [see Glossary]
25 ml red wine vinegar
1 tsp caster sugar

It is important to use freshly preserved lemon rind, which is not overly salty and still has some bite to the texture.

1 Place pumpkin in a bowl, drizzle with 1 tbsp olive oil, season to taste with sea salt and toss to combine. Char-grill or barbecue pumpkin over a low heat, turning occasionally, for 20 minutes or until pumpkin is tender, then cool slightly.
2 Place warm pumpkin, preserved lemon rind, olives and feta in a bowl. Combine vinegar, sugar and remaining olive oil in a screw-top jar and season to taste with freshly ground black pepper. Drizzle dressing over pumpkin salad and serve at room temperature.
Serves 6-8 as a starter

WITLOF, WALNUT AND PARSLEY SALAD

6 witlof [about 600g],
  trimmed, leaves separated
60 g walnut halves, roasted
  and coarsely chopped
40 g mild blue cheese, crumbled
⅓ cup [loosely packed] flat-leaf parsley leaves
¼ cup walnut oil
1½ tbsp sherry vinegar [see page 15]

1 Place witlof leaves on a large platter and scatter with chopped walnuts, cheese and parsley.
2 To serve, whisk walnut oil and vinegar in a small bowl, season to taste and pour over salad.
Serves 6 as a starter or accompaniment

RED LEAF SALAD WITH RADISH, BUFFALO MOZZARELLA FRITTERS AND ANCHOVY SAUCE

3 radishes, trimmed

1 radicchio, outer leaves discarded, leaves separated

100 g baby spinach

80 g Ligurian olives, or other small black olives, pitted [see page 241]

Olive oil

ANCHOVY SAUCE

50 g tin Ortiz anchovies, drained, oil reserved [see Glossary]

1 tbsp lemon juice

1 small clove of garlic, finely chopped

2 tbsp olive oil

MOZZARELLA FRITTERS

120 g [2 cups] breadcrumbs, made from day-old sourdough bread

2 tbsp coarsely chopped flat-leaf parsley, plus extra leaves, to serve

2 tbsp coarsely chopped basil

1 tsp finely grated lemon rind

4 buffalo mozzarella [about 110g each], each torn into 4 pieces [see Glossary]

Plain flour, seasoned to taste, for dusting

1 egg, lightly beaten

1 For anchovy sauce, process drained anchovies, lemon juice and garlic in a small food processor until smooth. Gradually add reserved anchovy oil and olive oil, drop by drop at first, then in a thin, steady stream until mixture is thick and emulsified. Add 1 tbsp boiling water, season to taste with freshly ground black pepper and combine well. Makes about ½ cup.

2 For mozzarella fritters, place breadcrumbs, herbs and lemon rind in a bowl, season to taste and combine well. Dust torn mozzarella in seasoned flour, shaking off excess, then dip in beaten egg, allowing excess to drain off, then coat in breadcrumb mixture, pressing crumbs to adhere. Place on a baking paper-lined tray and refrigerate until just before cooking.

3 Using a mandolin or sharp knife, cut radishes as thinly as possible, then place in a bowl of iced water and stand for 10 minutes.

4 Heat 1cm of olive oil in a heavy-based frying pan and cook mozzarella fritters, in batches, over medium-high heat, turning for 2-3 minutes or until crisp and golden. Drain on absorbent paper.

5 Place radicchio leaves on a platter. Add mozzarella fritters, scatter with spinach leaves and radish. Serve immediately, drizzled with anchovy sauce.

Serves 4 as a light meal

POTATO, CELERY, QUAIL EGG AND MINT SALAD

POTATO, CELERY, QUAIL EGG AND MINT SALAD

600 g small chat potatoes
12 quail eggs or 6 pullet eggs [see page 222]
2 tbsp mint leaves, torn
1 celery heart, tender leaves reserved, cut into 2mm-thick slices

SHERRY VINAIGRETTE
1 large clove of garlic, finely chopped
1 tsp Dijon mustard
1 tbsp sherry vinegar [see page 15]
100 ml extra-virgin olive oil

1 For sherry vinaigrette, combine garlic, mustard, vinegar and ½ tsp sea salt in a small bowl and whisk until well combined, then gradually whisk in oil until incorporated and season to taste with freshly ground black pepper. Makes about ½ cup.
2 Place potatoes in a saucepan, cover with water, bring to the boil and simmer until just tender, then drain. While still hot, drizzle potatoes with dressing and cool.
3 Place quail eggs in a saucepan, cover with cold water, bring to the boil and cook for 1 minute, then drain and peel under cold running water.
4 Halve quail eggs, add to potatoes with remaining ingredients and toss gently to combine.
Serves 8 as an accompaniment or light meal

SICILIAN CELERY HEART AND GREEN OLIVE SALAD

2 heads of celery
200 g Sicilian green olives, cracked and pitted [see Glossary]
100 g pecorino pepato [see page 222], shaved
Extra-virgin olive oil
1 tsp red wine vinegar

1 Remove outer stalks of celery and reserve for another use. Remove and reserve leaves and very small stalks from celery heart, then separate remaining stalks and wash well. Using a small knife or vegetable peeler, remove stringy fibres from larger stalks then, using a mandolin or vegetable peeler, shave celery stalks into 3mm-thick slices on the diagonal.

2 Place shaved celery, olives, half the shaved pecorino and reserved celery leaves and small stalks in a bowl, season to taste and combine well. Transfer to a large shallow bowl, drizzle generously with olive oil, then sprinkle with red wine vinegar and scatter with remaining shaved pecorino. Serve immediately.
Serves 8 as an accompaniment

SOFT-BOILED EGG AND ASPARAGUS SALAD WITH ANCHOVIES AND GREEN OLIVE DRESSING

400 g kipfler potatoes

3 bunches of young asparagus [about 32 spears]

8 eggs

5 cups [3 punnets] baby watercress

16 anchovy fillets

GREEN OLIVE DRESSING

1 cup gordal olives, pitted [see Glossary]

1 clove of garlic, finely chopped

Finely grated rind of ½ lemon

Juice of 1 lemon [about ¼ cup]

½ cup extra-virgin olive oil

1 tbsp brandy

1 For green olive dressing, process olives, garlic and lemon rind and juice in a food processor for 5-10 seconds or until coarsely chopped. Add oil and brandy, pulse to combine, then season to taste. Makes about 1¼ cups.

2 Wash kipflers and place in a heavy-based saucepan with enough cold water to cover. Bring to the boil over high heat and cook for 10-12 minutes. Drain, then peel potatoes while still warm and cut into 1.5cm rounds.

3 Meanwhile, bring 2 litres lightly salted water to the boil in a saucepan and cook asparagus for 2 minutes, drain, refresh in iced water, then drain again.

4 Bring 1.5 litres water to the boil in a saucepan. Add eggs and cook over high heat for 6½ minutes, then remove and cool eggs under cold running water to stop the cooking process. Peel eggs and cut in half.

5 To serve, divide half the watercress among plates, top with potatoes and half the asparagus, then spoon half the dressing over. Arrange halved eggs, anchovies, remaining asparagus and watercress on top and drizzle remaining dressing over.

Serves 4-6 as a starter or light meal

FRITTATA SALAD

3 large egg tomatoes, each cut into 8 wedges, then halved widthways

50 g kalamata olives, flattened and pitted

Olive oil

1 small cos, leaves washed and torn into bite-size pieces

2 Lebanese cucumbers, peeled, seeded and chopped

1 tbsp balsamic vinegar

FRITTATA

4 eggs, lightly beaten

3 green onions, thinly sliced

250 g [1 cup] firm ricotta

¼ cup mint, finely chopped

1 Place tomatoes and olives on an oven tray, drizzle with olive oil and season to taste, then roast at 180C for 30 minutes.

2 Meanwhile, for frittata, whisk together all ingredients until well combined, then season to taste. Heat a 26cm heavy-based ovenproof pan until hot, add 1 tbsp olive oil and swirl to coat base and side of pan with oil. Add egg mixture and cook over medium-high heat until a crust forms and frittata is half-cooked, then transfer to a 180C oven and cook for another 8-10 minutes or until set. Cool frittata for 5 minutes, then turn out onto a chopping board and cut into 2-3cm squares.

3 Combine remaining ingredients and 2 tbsp olive oil in a large bowl, add half the frittata pieces, and half the tomatoes and olives, and toss gently to combine. Divide salad among 4 plates and serve topped with remaining frittata, tomatoes and olives.

Serves 4

legumes, grains & pasta

Build a salad around pasta, beans, lentils, rice or one of the other good grains and you have substance and savour enough for it to stand alone as a complete meal, add class to basic barbecued beef, lamb or sausages, or – for vegetarian salads – to star as part of a larger vegetarian extravaganza. Salads like these are not only good for you, perfect for a crowd and relatively economical, but now that the former 'foods of the poor' have been rediscovered as a great way to eat, they're favourites with top chefs and hosts who know that satisfying peasant food is the smart thing to serve.

You can cook beans [which include chickpeas] or lentils, barley and rice ahead of time. Simply store cooked beans or lentils in a covered bowl in the refrigerator. Spread cooked barley or rice on an oiled tray to cool, gently separating any lumps with your fingers, then refrigerate in a covered container. Any of these can be reheated by steaming – this is better than microwaving because it heats more evenly. You can also use canned beans or chickpeas, draining them into a sieve, rinsing them well and draining again before using.

legume, grain & pasta varieties

BORLOTTI BEANS [1]
Much used in Italian cooking, borlotti beans are meaty flavoured and smooth textured.

ORZO [2]
Tiny pasta shapes resembling rice grains. Also called risoni.

QUINOA [3]
An exceptionally nutritious grain native to the Andes and cultivated in that region for more than 5000 years. It is not a true cereal grain but the seed of a plant distantly related to spinach; it looks a little like millet and has a light, delicate taste. It cooks quickly to a light, fluffy texture.

PEARL BARLEY [4]
Barley grains which have had the husk removed and have been steamed and polished. Pearl barley has a robust, nutty flavour.

FARRO [5]
The polished grains of the Tuscan cereal [*Triticum dicoccum* Schubler], which look and taste a little like brown rice, but with oat- and barley-like undertones. The name farro or faro is sometimes used, erroneously, for the ancient grain spelt [*Triticum spelta*], an ancestor of modern wheat.

DRIED LIMA BEANS [6]
Also known as butter beans, limas are available large or small. They have a mild flavour and smooth texture and are especially good in salads.

FRENCH-STYLE GREEN LENTILS [7]
The small, dark, blue-green lentils grown in the Le Puy district in southern France have long been considered the aristocrats of their kind. No longer imported into Australia for quarantine reasons, the locally grown varieties, though slightly smaller, are as good and are less expensive. They are sold as Australian green lentils.

BLACK-EYE BEANS [8]
Really a white bean with the characteristic black spot. A great favourite in southern USA, where they are eaten both fresh and dried, but known in this country only in their dried form. Mild in flavour, they go well with rich sauces and meats.

CASARECCI [9]
Pasta shapes formed from 6-7cm-long flat noodles, twisted together in pairs.

POLENTA [10]
The staple cereal of northern Italy, polenta is cornmeal ground to various degrees of fineness, and is prepared by boiling with water to make a porridge. It can be eaten like this, or spread out, chilled to firm it, then grilled.

BLACK TURTLE BEANS [11]
Small, black dried beans with a deliciously savoury flavour.

CHICKPEAS
Really a dried bean, with a warm flavour and crisp texture, perfect in salads, soups and stews. Available both in bulk and, cooked, in cans.

BASMATI RICE
Long-grained rice with wonderfully nutty fragrance and flavour, originally [and still] imported from Pakistan, but now also grown in Australia. Basmati should always be cooked by the absorption method, rather than in lots of water, so that you don't throw any of that lovely flavour down the sink.

RED KIDNEY BEANS
Full-flavoured, mealy dried beans. Available both in bulk and, cooked, in cans.

ROASTED VEGETABLE SALAD WITH OLIVE AND CAPER DRESSING AND CRISP POLENTA

100 g instant polenta

350 g bulb of fennel, trimmed
and cut into thin wedges

400 g orange sweet potato, halved
lengthways and cut into thin wedges

4 cloves of garlic, unpeeled
Extra-virgin olive oil

450 g baby beetroot, trimmed

150 g small green beans, trimmed
Peanut or canola oil

125 g [2 cups] wild rocket

OLIVE AND CAPER DRESSING

120 g Ligurian olives, pitted
and coarsely chopped

1 tbsp baby capers, rinsed and drained

1 tbsp coarsely chopped mint

1 tbsp coarsely chopped flat-leaf parsley

1 tbsp lemon juice

⅓ cup extra-virgin olive oil

1 Bring 2 cups water and 2 tsp salt to the boil in a heavy-based saucepan, then, whisking continuously, add polenta in a thin, steady stream until mixture returns to the boil. Using a wooden spoon, stir polenta over low heat for 3-4 minutes or until very thick. Pour polenta into a lightly greased 20cm-square cake tin, then cool and refrigerate until set.

2 For olive and caper dressing, combine all ingredients in a bowl, season to taste and mix well. Makes about ¾ cup.

3 Combine fennel, sweet potato and garlic in a large roasting pan with 2 tbsp olive oil and season to taste. Wrap beetroot in foil and place in a separate roasting pan, then roast vegetables, turning once, at 200C for 30-35 minutes or until fennel and sweet potato are golden and beetroot is tender.

4 Meanwhile, cook beans in boiling salted water until just tender, drain, refresh in iced water, then drain again.

5 Peel and halve beetroot if large, then combine with 2 tbsp olive and caper dressing.

6 Just before serving, cut polenta into 2x5cm pieces and deep-fry, in batches, in hot oil until crisp and golden, then drain on absorbent paper. Combine polenta with roasted vegetables, peeled garlic cloves, beans, rocket and half the remaining dressing and mix gently. Serve immediately, drizzled with remaining dressing.

Serves 4

OLIVES

Hailing from the Italian Riviera, Ligurian olives are tiny black olives with a sweet and delicate buttery flavour. They are made from taggiasche olives, a variety originally cultivated by Benedictine monks living near the Ligurian town of Taggia. High in oil, they are used for both eating and making oil. If unavailable, substitute with other small black olives such as Niçoise, which are a close cousin to Ligurian olives and are grown in Provence, along the neighbouring French Riviera. Ligurian and Niçoise olives are available from Italian delicatessens and some greengrocers.

PANCETTA, PEA, LENTIL AND MINT SALAD

225 g French-style green lentils [see page 238]
2 small onions, finely chopped
300 g piece of pancetta or speck, chopped [see Glossary]
150 g baby green beans, trimmed
200 g sugar snap peas, trimmed
350 g peas, podded
2½ tbsp lemon juice
100 ml olive oil
¼ cup coarsely chopped mint

1 Place lentils and onions in a large saucepan, cover with plenty of water and bring to the boil, then simmer over medium heat for 30-35 minutes or until lentils are tender. Drain, then transfer to a large bowl.
2 Meanwhile, add pancetta to a hot non-stick frying pan and cook, stirring occasionally, over medium heat for 5-8 minutes or until browned.
3 Cook baby green beans in a saucepan of boiling salted water for 2 minutes, then add sugar snap peas and peas and cook for another 2-3 minutes or until peas and beans are tender, then drain. Add beans, peas and pancetta to lentils with remaining ingredients, season to taste and toss well to combine.
Serves 4

WARM CASARECCI WITH BROCCOLINI AND ROSEMARY SALAD

400 g casarecci [see page 238], fusilli or farfalle
Extra-virgin olive oil
4 cloves of garlic, finely chopped
½ tsp dried chilli flakes, or to taste
1 tbsp finely chopped rosemary
2 bunches of broccolini, trimmed
Grated rind of 1 lemon
¼ cup lemon juice, or to taste
50 g shaved pecorino
40 g pistachios, coarsely chopped

1 Cook pasta in plenty of boiling salted water until al dente, drain, refresh in iced water, then drain again. Transfer pasta to a large bowl.
2 Meanwhile, heat 100ml olive oil in a heavy-based frying pan over medium heat, add garlic, chilli and rosemary and cook for 30 seconds or until fragrant. Add broccolini, lemon rind and juice and stir to combine, then cook over medium heat for 2-3 minutes or until broccolini is just tender.
3 Add broccolini mixture, half the pecorino and pistachios to pasta and toss gently to combine. Divide among bowls, drizzle with a little olive oil and serve topped with remaining pecorino.
Serves 4-6

PANCETTA, PEA, LENTIL AND MINT SALAD

BORLOTTI BEAN, COTECHINO AND PROVOLONE SALAD WITH MINT DRESSING AND CHAR-GRILLED CHILLI

750 ml red wine

1 cotechino sausage [see Glossary], about 500g

2 fresh long red chillies

Olive oil

400 g [2 cups] dried borlotti beans, soaked in cold water overnight [discarding any that float to the surface], then drained

1 dried bay leaf

4 sprigs of thyme

2 cloves of garlic, peeled and bruised

8 white peppercorns

100 g [4 cups] baby rocket

150 g provolone piccante [see Glossary], shaved, to serve

MINT DRESSING

¾ cup coarsely chopped mint

½ cup coarsely chopped parsley

¼ cup cabernet sauvignon vinegar

⅓ cup lemon juice

Finely grated rind of ½ lemon

1 clove of garlic, finely chopped

1 cup extra-virgin olive oil

This recipe is best started 1 day in advance by soaking the beans and cooking the cotechino.

1 Bring red wine and 1 litre water to the boil in a heavy-based saucepan, add cotechino, ensuring it is totally immersed in the liquid, then simmer over low-medium heat for 3 hours. Remove cotechino from pan and cool. Discard cooking liquid.

2 Brush chillies with ¼ tsp oil, then cook, turning, on a barbecue or char-grill for 2-3 minutes or until chillies are blistered and charred all over. Place in a bowl, cover with plastic wrap and set aside.

3 Meanwhile, place drained borlotti beans, bay leaf, thyme, garlic, peppercorns and 2 litres cold water in a large heavy-based saucepan, cover and bring to boil. Uncover and simmer over low-medium heat for 20-25 minutes or until beans are tender. Drain and spread on a tray to cool.

4 Peel, seed and coarsely chop chillies, then combine with 2 tbsp olive oil and season to taste.

5 For mint dressing, combine all ingredients in a large bowl and season to taste. Makes 1½ cups. When beans have cooled to room temperature, stir in dressing.

6 Cut cotechino into 5mm-thick slices. Heat 2 tsp olive oil in a large non-stick frying pan, add cotechino and cook over high heat for 3-4 minutes or until crisp, then turn and cook for another 1-2 minutes. Drain on absorbent paper.

7 To serve, divide half the rocket among 4 shallow bowls, spoon over half the bean mixture and cotechino, then repeat layering with remaining rocket, bean mixture and cotechino. Top with char-grilled chillies and scatter with shaved provolone.

Serves 4

WARM SALAD OF PRAWNS, BROAD BEANS AND RED RICE

300 g podded broad beans
[about 750g unpodded]

200 g red rice [1 cup, see note below]

Olive oil

1 onion, finely chopped

2 cloves of garlic, finely chopped

50 g sliced prosciutto, chopped

12 jumbo green prawns, heads removed, cleaned, leaving tails intact, and halved lengthways

ANCHOVY AND PARSLEY VINAIGRETTE

10 anchovy fillets

¼ cup extra-virgin olive oil

1 tbsp lemon juice

⅓ cup coarsely chopped flat-leaf parsley

1 For anchovy and parsley vinaigrette, process anchovies in the small bowl of a food processor until smooth, then gradually add oil until well combined and emulsified. Stir in lemon juice and parsley and combine well. Makes about ⅓ cup.

2 Cook broad beans in boiling salted water for 2-3 minutes or until just tender, drain, refresh in iced water, then drain again and peel.

3 Cook red rice in plenty of boiling water for 20 minutes or until just tender but still firm to the bite, then drain well and place in a large bowl.

4 Meanwhile, heat 2 tbsp olive oil in a frying pan, add onion and garlic and cook for 6-8 minutes or until soft. Add onion mixture, broad beans and prosciutto to cooked rice, stir in anchovy and parsley vinaigrette, then season to taste, combine well and stand for 1 hour to allow flavours to develop.

5 Just before serving, brush cut sides of prawns lightly with oil, season to taste and char-grill or barbecue, cut-side down, for 2 minutes, then turn and cook for another minute. Place prawns over red rice salad and serve immediately.

Serves 6-8

RED RICE

As the name implies, red rice is a rice variety with a red-brown bran layer. It is grown in the Camargue marshlands of southern France and is prized for its aesthetic appeal, nutty flavour and firm texture. Red rice cooks more quickly than brown rice and can be used in any of the same recipes. During cooking, the red hue fades into a beige-pink colour.

As with brown rice, this is a highly nutritious variety, rich in fibre and B-group vitamins. It has become more popular with Australian chefs in recent years, and is now available in select delicatessens and grocers.

SAFFRON AND COUSCOUS SALAD

SAFFRON AND COUSCOUS SALAD

Olive oil

1 large Spanish onion,
   halved and thinly sliced

2 tbsp tomato paste

1 tsp each ground cumin, ground
   coriander and ground cinnamon

¼ tsp saffron threads [see Glossary]

400 g [2 cups] instant couscous

½ cup coarsely chopped flat-leaf parsley

125 g fresh dates [about 6],
   pitted and thinly sliced

⅓ cup freshly squeezed orange juice

¼ cup freshly squeezed lemon juice

40 g flaked almonds, roasted

Flat breads and Greek-style
   yoghurt, to serve

1 Heat 2 tbsp olive oil in a heavy-based saucepan, add onion and cook, stirring occasionally, over medium heat for 8 minutes or until soft. Add tomato paste and ground spices and stir for another 5 minutes or until fragrant. Add saffron, 1½ tsp sea salt, 400ml water and bring to the boil. Remove from heat, stir in couscous and stand, covered, for 10 minutes or until liquid is absorbed.

2 Add remaining ingredients, except almonds, and ⅓ cup olive oil to couscous and fluff with a fork to combine. Scatter salad with almonds and serve with flat breads and Greek-style yoghurt.
Serves 4-6 as an accompaniment

CHICKPEA AND RICE SALAD

Olive oil

2 shallots, finely chopped

1 fresh small green chilli, finely chopped

1 tsp ground allspice

300 g [1½ cups] basmati rice, rinsed

2 400g cans chickpeas,
   drained and rinsed well

1 small clove of garlic, finely chopped

2 tbsp cider vinegar

1 bunch of chives, cut into 2cm lengths

3 green onions, trimmed to
   25cm and finely chopped

⅓ cup chopped coriander

1 cup chopped rocket [about ½ bunch]

1 Heat 2 tbsp olive oil in a large saucepan or deep frying pan, add shallots, chilli and 1 tsp salt and cook, stirring occasionally, over medium heat for 5 minutes. Add allspice, rice and chickpeas and stir for 1 minute or until rice is lightly toasted. Add 2¾ cups boiling water, bring to the boil, cover and cook over low heat for 12 minutes or until most of the liquid has been absorbed. Transfer rice mixture to a large bowl and cool for 20 minutes.
2 Meanwhile, whisk together garlic, vinegar and 2 tbsp olive oil in a small bowl and season to taste. Stir dressing into rice mixture with chives, green onion and coriander and serve with chopped rocket.
Serves 8 as an accompaniment

GRILLED CUTTLEFISH AND CHICKPEA SALAD

1.5 kg cuttlefish, cleaned, tentacles
  reserved and hoods cut open
  Extra-virgin olive oil
  2 cloves of garlic, finely chopped
  2 Spanish onions, sliced into 5mm-wide rings
  6 dried small red chillies
1½ tsp smoked Spanish paprika
  2 tsp dried oregano
  ¼ tsp saffron threads [see Glossary]
  ¼ tsp cayenne
  1 cup freshly squeezed orange juice
  1 tbsp lemon juice
400 g can chickpeas, rinsed and drained
  1 bunch of coriander,
  leaves picked and chopped

1 Brush cuttlefish tentacles and hoods with olive oil, then char-grill or barbecue over high heat for 40 seconds on each side or until just opaque [large tentacles will take slightly longer to cook]. Cool cuttlefish, then cut hoods into thick slices and place in a large bowl with tentacles.

2 Heat ¼ cup olive oil in a saucepan, add garlic, onions and whole dried chillies and stir over medium heat for 3 minutes or until onions are just soft. Add paprika, oregano, saffron and cayenne, stir for 2 minutes, then add orange and lemon juices and bring to the boil. Remove from heat and cool slightly. Pour mixture over cuttlefish, add chickpeas, then season to taste and combine well. Cool to room temperature, stir in chopped coriander and serve.

Serves 6 as a light meal

BLACK BEAN AND KIDNEY BEAN SALAD

200 g [1 cup] dried black turtle beans,
    soaked in cold water overnight

1 head of garlic, halved widthways, plus
3 extra cloves of garlic, peeled

400 g [2 cups] dried red kidney beans,
    soaked in cold water overnight

4 cooked corn cobs, kernels cut from cobs

1 fresh red serrano chilli, seeded
    and finely chopped [see Glossary]

½ cup lemon juice

½ cup olive oil

2 tbsp red wine vinegar

1 Spanish onion, finely chopped

1½ tsp ground cumin

1 cup [loosely packed] torn coriander leaves

1 Place drained black beans and halved garlic in a large saucepan, add plenty of water and bring to the boil, then simmer over medium heat for 30 minutes. Add drained kidney beans and cook for another hour or until tender. Drain, discard garlic and place beans in a large bowl with corn.

2 Combine 2 tsp sea salt and extra garlic in a mortar and, using a pestle, pound to a fine paste. Transfer paste to a small bowl, add remaining ingredients except coriander, and whisk to combine. Pour over salad, toss to combine, then stand for 15 minutes for flavours to develop. Stir in coriander and serve.

Serves 8 as an accompaniment

CORN

When buying corn, it is important to select the youngest ears available, as corn is one of a few vegetables which converts sugar to starch after picking, so older corn is less sweet and tougher than freshly picked cobs. To choose fresh corn, only buy whole ears, and then peel back the husks (which should be a strong green colour), and check the kernels, which should be plump, even-sized and round. To remove kernels from the cob, remove the husk and any silks, then stand the cob upright on a chopping board and, using a sharp paring knife, cut down each side of the cob, starting at the base of the kernel.

BARLEY, LAMB AND GRAPE SALAD ON LETTUCE

2 tsp sumac [see Glossary]

2 tsp coriander seeds, dry-roasted and crushed

2 tsp ground cumin

¼ tsp ground allspice

2 cloves of garlic, finely chopped

½ cup lemon juice

100 ml olive oil

4 lamb backstraps [about 240g each]

100 g Italian pearl barley [see Glossary]

1 bunch of flat-leaf parsley, leaves picked and torn if large

1 bunch of spearmint, leaves picked and torn

350 g green seedless grapes, quartered

Cos lettuce leaves, to serve

1 Place half of each of the spices and garlic in a bowl, add 1 tbsp lemon juice and 2 tbsp olive oil and stir to form a paste. Place lamb in a flat glass or ceramic dish, rub with spice mixture, then cover and refrigerate for 2 hours.

2 Cook barley in boiling water for 25 minutes or until tender, then drain, refresh in iced water and drain again.

3 Char-grill or barbecue lamb for 2-3 minutes on each side for medium-rare or until cooked to your liking. Cool to room temperature before cutting into thin slices.

4 Place barley, herbs and grapes in a bowl and toss gently to combine. Place remaining spices, garlic, lemon juice and olive oil in a bowl and whisk to combine well, then pour over salad and toss gently to combine. Serve salad spooned onto lettuce leaves, topped with lamb.

Serves 4-6

FARRO SALAD WITH RADICCHIO AND ANCHOVIES

250 g [1½ cups] cracked grain farro [see page 238]

1 radicchio, tough outer leaves discarded, finely shredded

5 cups picked watercress sprigs, chopped

12 anchovy fillets in olive oil, drained and halved lengthways

2 tbsp oil from anchovies

1 clove of garlic, finely chopped

⅓ cup extra-virgin olive oil

¼ cup red wine vinegar

120 g [1¼ cups] shaved pecorino

1 Cook farro in boiling water for 30 minutes or until tender, then drain well and cool.

2 Toss farro with remaining ingredients in a large bowl, season to taste and serve immediately.

Serves 6-8

BARLEY, LAMB AND GRAPE SALAD ON LETTUCE

AROMATIC BAKED BEANS

150 g dried lima beans, soaked in
    cold water overnight, then drained

2 tbsp olive oil

1 large onion, halved and thinly sliced

2 cloves of garlic, chopped

1 large carrot, thinly sliced

6 sprigs of thyme

½ tsp ground allspice

2 dried bay leaves

400 g can chopped tomatoes

Extra-virgin olive oil, to serve

1 Cook beans in plenty of boiling water for 25 minutes or until about half-cooked, then drain well.

2 Heat olive oil in a casserole, add onion, garlic, carrot, thyme, allspice and bay leaves and stir over medium heat for 5 minutes or until onion is soft. Add drained beans and tomatoes, cover tightly with foil, then cook at 180C for 1 hour or until beans are soft and liquid is absorbed. Cool beans to room temperature, season to taste and serve drizzled with extra-virgin olive oil. Beans will keep, refrigerated, in an airtight container, for up to 5 days.

Serves 6

EGGPLANT, TOMATO, ZUCCHINI AND QUINOA SALAD WITH PINENUTS

Olive oil

250 g [1¼ cups] quinoa, rinsed
    under running water [see Glossary]

2 Lebanese eggplant, cut into
    6mm-thick rounds [see Glossary]

2 zucchini, cut into 6mm-thick rounds

2 tsp ground cumin

1 tsp coriander seeds, finely crushed

2 tbsp lime juice

⅓ cup coarsely chopped coriander

1 large ripe tomato, seeded and chopped

60 g pinenuts, roasted

1 Heat 1 tbsp olive oil in a saucepan, add quinoa and stir over medium heat for 2 minutes or until lightly toasted. Add 700ml water and 1 tsp salt and bring to the boil, then reduce heat to low and cook, covered, for 12-15 minutes or until most of the liquid has been absorbed. Drain off any remaining liquid and set aside.

2 Meanwhile, combine eggplant, zucchini, cumin, crushed coriander and 2 tbsp olive oil in a roasting pan and season to taste, then roast at 200C for 20 minutes or until vegetables are tender and golden.

3 Transfer hot vegetables to a large bowl, add remaining ingredients, 2 tbsp olive oil and quinoa and toss gently to combine. Serve warm or at room temperature.

Serves 4-6 as a light meal

ORZO, ZUCCHINI AND MINT SALAD

400 g orzo [see Glossary]

Olive oil

3 green and 3 yellow
zucchini, thinly sliced widthways

1 clove of garlic, finely chopped

1½ tsp fennel seeds, coarsely crushed

50 g [⅓ cup] currants, covered with boiling
water, soaked for 5 minutes, then drained

1 cup [loosely packed] mint
leaves, coarsely chopped

1½ tbsp white balsamic condiment
or white wine vinegar [see page 15]

1 Cook orzo in boiling salted water for 10 minutes or until al dente, drain, refresh in iced water and drain again.
2 Meanwhile, heat 1 tbsp olive oil in a large frying pan, add half the zucchini and ½ tsp sea salt and toss over high heat for 3 minutes or until zucchini are just tender. Transfer zucchini to a bowl, then repeat with another tablespoon of oil, remaining zucchini and another ½ tsp sea salt, adding garlic and fennel seeds just before zucchini are cooked.
3 Combine orzo, zucchini, ¼ cup olive oil and remaining ingredients in a bowl and season to taste with freshly ground black pepper and a little more sea salt, if necessary.
Serves 6-8 as an accompaniment

ROMAN BEANS, WHITE BEANS AND PINENUTS WITH ANCHOVY DRESSING

200 g [1 cup] dried great northern
white beans, soaked in cold
water overnight, then drained

500 g Roman [flat green] beans, topped

ANCHOVY DRESSING

¼ cup extra-virgin olive oil

4 anchovy fillets, finely chopped

1 small clove of garlic, finely chopped

1½ tbsp lemon juice

50 g pinenuts, roasted

1 Cover drained white beans with water and bring to the boil, simmer for 35 minutes or until tender, then drain and place in a bowl.
2 Cook Roman beans in boiling salted water until just tender, drain and refresh in iced water, then drain again. Cut into 4cm pieces on the diagonal and add to white beans.
3 For anchovy dressing, place oil, anchovies and garlic in a small frying pan and heat slowly over low heat for 2-3 minutes or until oil is hot. Add lemon juice and pinenuts, season to taste, then pour over beans and toss to combine.
Serves 6-8 as an accompaniment

ORZO, ZUCCHINI AND MINT SALAD

fruit

You're already halfway to a beautiful dessert when you start with the wonderful tastes and textures of fresh fruits. All that is needed is to glorify them with fragrant syrups and delectable accompaniments, from delicate pastries to creamy fresh curds. These are the right desserts for the way we live today, unfussy to make and refreshingly light at the end of a good meal.

Although many of the recipes in this chapter are meant for summer, there are cool-weather inspirations, too, such as fruits baked in port and a heady, herb-scented salad for the winter citrus crop [omit figs if they're out of season]. And you can apply some ideas given here to fruits of other seasons. Pears, instead of plums, would be delicious poached in prosecco and served with spice-scented quark, and the rosewater meringues would be a delight with that current chefs' darling, rhubarb, or with strawberries, which are available almost year-round. With these, you might like to sandwich the meringues together in pairs with cream and serve them beside the fruit. For this, gently press the base of each meringue, while still warm, to make a hollow, then replace upside down on the baking tray and return to the turned-off oven to cool.

fruit varieties

APPLES [1]

The tart-sweet granny smith is unrivalled for cooking and excellent as an eating apple too. Lady Williams are flavoursome and crisp. Sundowner is a little less firm but very sweet. Royal gala is small to medium-size, with sweet, juicy flesh.

PEARS [2, 3]

The long-established queen of cooking, pears have dense flesh and are juicy. The spicy beurre bosc is also excellent for salads or the cheeseboard. Small, brilliantly sunset-coloured corellas are equally good when hard and crunchy or ripe and juicy.

NECTARINES [4], PEACHES [7]

Choose nectarines and peaches by scent, not by skin colour. White ones are the most gloriously perfumed. Leave nectarines and peaches at room temperature until fully ripe, then refrigerate.

PAWPAW [5], PAPAYA [8]

Confusion over the name of this fruit stems from the two varieties being sold, side by side, under different names. The more elongated pink-fleshed type is typically sold as papaya [8], while the larger orange-fleshed variety is usually sold as pawpaw [5]. In fact, both are the same fruit.

RAMBUTANS [6]

Native to the Malay peninsula, but now grown here. Similar to lychees in both flavour and texture, but not as sweet.

BERRIES [9, 11]

Some strawberries are delicious, some hardly worth eating – choose those with good aroma and no white showing at the stem end. Raspberries [11], blackberries and blueberries [9] should smell fresh with no hint of mustiness.

FIGS [10]

Ripe figs may be purple, brownish or green. They should be soft, strongly coloured for the variety and sweet-smelling. They are highly perishable so refrigerate for only a day or two.

PLUMS [12]

In general, choose large, soft plums for eating and smaller, firm ones for cooking. Their skins should still have the bloom on them and be free of brown patches, which indicate sunburn and affect the flavour.

BETHONGA GOLD PINEAPPLE

The exclusive product of one Queensland grower, Bethonga Golds have intense, sweet flavour, low acidity and crisp golden flesh. They are labelled with their name.

BLOOD ORANGES

The characteristic red streaking of both skin and flesh in blood oranges is more pronounced if they are grown in a cool climate. They are sweeter than other oranges.

CHERRIES

Cherries should be shiny and fat – small ones may have been picked early and be lacking in flavour. Sour varieties, if you can get them, are the classic choice for European recipes such as black forest cake.

LIMES

More piercing in flavour than lemons, limes also thrive better in hot climates, so they go naturally with Asian and other tropical cuisines.

LYCHEES

Native to China but now grown here, lychees taste rather like more luscious, perfumed grapes.

MELONS

Rockmelon should have a clean scar where the stem was, showing that it was ripe when picked. Honeydew is ripe when the skin is creamy rather than white. A ripe watermelon sounds hollow when tapped; if it is already cut, choose a piece with richly coloured flesh. The mini lee melon is a small, round watermelon and is seedless – that is, it will have a few small white seeds and perhaps the odd black one.

MEYER LEMONS

Thin-skinned, round lemons, sweeter than other varieties and very aromatic.

MIXED BERRY SALAD WITH ROSEWATER MERINGUES

MIXED BERRY SALAD WITH ROSEWATER MERINGUES

150 g raspberries

150 g blueberries

250 g strawberries, halved

150 g blackberries

2 tbsp lime juice

Finely grated rind of ½ lime

65 g [¼ cup] grated light palm sugar [see Glossary]

ROSEWATER MERINGUES

2 eggwhites

110 g [½ cup] caster sugar

1 tsp rosewater

1 Combine all the berries in a bowl. Whisk together lime juice, rind and sugar until sugar dissolves. Pour mixture over berries, toss gently to combine and set aside for 1 hour for flavours to develop.
2 For rosewater meringues, using an electric mixer, beat eggwhites until frothy, gradually add sugar, 2 tbsp at a time, beating until sugar dissolves before adding the next addition, and beat until mixture is stiff and glossy. Beat in rosewater until combined. Place tablespoonfuls of meringue onto baking-paper-lined oven trays and bake at 120C for 1 hour, or until crisp. Turn off oven and cool meringues in oven with door ajar. Makes about 30. Meringues will keep in an airtight container in a cool, dry place for up to 1 week.
3 Serve mixed berry salad with meringues passed separately.
Serves 6

BAKED PEARS, PLUMS AND APPLES IN PORT

4 small granny smith apples, halved

4 beurre bosc pears, halved

200 g caster sugar

1 cinnamon stick, crumbled

Juice and wide strips of rind from 1 lemon

180 ml tawny port

4 plums [about 500g], halved and stoned

1 Place apple and pear halves, flesh-side down, in a large ovenproof dish, scatter with sugar, cinnamon and lemon rind, then drizzle with lemon juice and port. Bake at 190C for 30 minutes, add plums and bake for another 10 minutes or until tender. Cool slightly, then serve.
Serves 4-6

PROSECCO-POACHED PLUMS WITH CARDAMOM QUARK

750 ml prosecco [see Glossary]

150 g [⅔ cup] caster sugar

1 wide strip of orange rind

¼ tsp cardamom seeds

36 mixed plum varieties [see below]

CARDAMOM QUARK

500 g quark [see Glossary]

40 g [¼ cup] icing sugar

1 tbsp orange juice

Finely grated rind of 1 orange

¼ tsp ground cardamom

1 For cardamom quark, combine all ingredients in a bowl, stir until smooth, then cover and refrigerate. Makes about 2½ cups.

2 Combine prosecco, sugar, orange rind and cardamom seeds in a large heavy-based saucepan and stir over medium heat until sugar dissolves, then bring to the boil. Reduce heat to low and simmer for 10 minutes. Add large plums and simmer gently for 4 minutes, then add small plums and simmer for another 3-4 minutes or until just soft. Using a slotted spoon, remove plums from syrup and, when cool enough to handle, peel skins from blood plums. Simmer cooking liquid over high heat until reduced by one-quarter and syrupy, then strain.

3 Serve plums warm or at room temperature with syrup poured over and cardamom quark to the side.

Serves 12

PLUMS

This recipe uses a combination of Angelina, blood and president plum varieties, to offer an appealing contrast in size, colour and flavour. Angelina plums are small, oval shaped plums with an extremely sweet flavour and crisp texture. They can be substituted with other small sugar plums like d'agen or moyers. Blood plums are dark red-fleshed, spicy Japanese plums such as satsumas and mariposas. President plums are a large, dark blue, orange-fleshed freestone plum originating in Europe. If unavailable, use other dark skinned plums like black amber or ausibelle. Use one variety of plum, or a mixture of plums and other stone fruit, including nectarines and peaches.

CITRUS SALAD IN WHITE WINE AND THYME SYRUP

2 blood oranges

2 ruby oranges

2 navel oranges

4 black or green figs, quartered

Double cream, optional, to serve

WINE SYRUP

250 ml riesling or other fruity white wine

330 g [1½ cups] caster sugar

Thinly peeled rind of ½ lemon

1 tbsp thyme leaves

1 For wine syrup, place wine, sugar, lemon rind and 1 cup water in a saucepan and stir over low heat until sugar dissolves, then bring to the boil and simmer over medium heat for 8-10 minutes or until syrupy. Discard rind, stir in thyme and cool to room temperature. Makes about 1½ cups.

2 Using a small knife, cut rind and pith from citrus, then cut fruit into wedges and place in a large bowl. Pour wine syrup over and toss gently to combine. Serve immediately topped with double cream, if using.

Serves 6

VARIATIONS

* The herbaceous, aromatic flavours of this syrup also work well with other fruit, especially stone fruit. Make double the quantity of syrup, add 4 nectarines and 4 white peaches and simmer for 10 minutes, then add 4 damsons or tegan blue plums and cook for another 2-3 minutes or until fruit is tender. Remove stone fruit, using a slotted spoon, then peel and return to syrup. Serve cooled stone fruit drizzled with syrup, with clotted cream to the side.

* Vary the winning combination of fruit and herbs by substituting 250ml rosé in place of the fruity white wine and use 2 bay leaves or lavender sprigs instead of thyme. Add torn bay leaves to syrup before bringing to the boil, to infuse the syrup with their flavour. Other citrus fruits, such as imperial mandarins, pink grapefruit and Valencia oranges, can also be used, peeled and cut into segments. Serve with whipped cream.

* Use wine syrup to brush over a semolina walnut cake. Beat 125g butter, ⅔ cup caster sugar and 2 tsp finely grated orange rind until pale and creamy. Add 4 eggs, beating after each, then stir in ½ cup each plain flour and fine semolina and 1 cup [finely ground] walnuts. Bake at 180C for 30 minutes or until a cake tester withdraws clean, then brush with warm wine syrup and cool. Serve with Greek-style yoghurt.

LAVENDER-POACHED STONE FRUIT WITH WALNUT AND HONEY-CREAM SANDWICHES

750 ml marsanne or other fruity white wine
330 g [1½ cups] caster sugar
Thinly peeled rind and juice of 1 orange
2 tsp dried lavender, tied in a piece of muslin
6 white nectarines
3 peaches, halved and stoned
12-18 apricots [depending on size]
WALNUT AND HONEY-CREAM SANDWICHES
2 tbsp honey
150 ml double cream
100 g walnuts, roasted and very finely chopped
6 brioche rolls [6cm diameter]
Icing sugar, for dusting

For an equally delicious but quite different flavour, substitute 6 large basil leaves for the lavender.

1 Place all ingredients, except stone fruit, and 1½ cups water in a large saucepan and bring to the boil. Add nectarines, cover with a round of baking paper, then a plate and cook over low heat for 5 minutes. Add peach halves and apricots, cover, and cook for another 15 minutes or until fruit is tender. Cool, then remove skins from stone fruit.
2 For walnut and honey-cream sandwiches, combine honey, cream and walnuts in a small bowl. Working with one brioche at a time, cut each into four horizontally and, using one quarter of the walnut and honey-cream, sandwich brioche together to re-form brioche, then repeat with remaining brioche and cream. Dust with icing sugar.
3 Serve stone fruit and syrup at room temperature or chilled, with halved brioche sandwiches.
Serves 6

PICNIC FRUIT SALAD

1 vanilla bean, halved lengthways
110 g [½ cup] caster sugar
4 peaches
4 white nectarines
150 g raspberries
⅓ cup lime or lemon juice
150 ml gin or vodka

The idea for this recipe comes from renowned British food writer Jane Grigson.

1 Place scraped seeds from vanilla bean in a bowl, then cut bean into 4cm lengths and combine with sugar.
2 Using a small knife, cut a small cross into skins at the base of stone fruit. Place stone fruit, one at a time, in boiling water for 30 seconds, then immediately refresh in iced water. Peel, cut in half and remove stones, then cut into quarters.
3 Layer stone fruit with raspberries in a 1.75-litre wide-mouthed thermos or tall plastic container with a lid, sprinkling with sugar mixture and lime juice as you go. Pour in gin, seal container and invert once, then refrigerate for several hours or overnight. Alternatively, transfer the fruit salad to a tall glass jug for serving.
Serves 4

LAVENDER-POACHED STONE FRUIT WITH WALNUT AND HONEY-CREAM SANDWICHES

TROPICAL FRUITS IN STAR ANISE AND CASSIA SYRUP

TROPICAL FRUITS IN STAR ANISE AND CASSIA SYRUP

165 g [¾ cup] caster sugar

4 cm piece of cassia bark [see Glossary]

4 star anise [see Glossary]

1 vanilla bean, halved lengthways

⅓ cup lime juice

4 large mangoes [about 2kg], peeled, seeded and cut into 2cm pieces

500 g lychees, peeled

1 pineapple (preferably Bethonga Gold), peeled, halved lengthways, cored and cut into 2cm pieces

1 red-fleshed pawpaw, peeled, seeded and cut into 2cm pieces

1 Combine sugar, 1½ cups water, spices, scraped seeds from vanilla bean and bean in a saucepan and stir over medium heat until sugar dissolves, then bring to the boil and simmer for 5 minutes. Remove from heat, stir in lime juice and cool for 10 minutes.

2 Meanwhile, combine fruit in a large bowl, pour warm syrup over, cool, then refrigerate until chilled before serving.

Serves 6-8

PINEAPPLE AND MINT IN ROSE AND CARDAMOM SYRUP

750 ml rosé

150 g (⅔ cup) caster sugar

12 cardamom pods, seeds removed and lightly crushed

1 large ripe pineapple (about 1.3kg), peeled and cored

½ cup mint leaves, torn

1 Combine 200ml wine, sugar and cardamom seeds in a saucepan and slowly bring to a simmer, stirring to dissolve sugar. Remove from heat, cool, then stir in remaining wine.

2 Cut pineapple into 2cm pieces, toss with mint leaves, then divide mixture among 6 tall 300ml glasses. Pour unstrained rosé and cardamom syrup over pineapple in glasses and serve.

Serves 6

I commend salad to all those who have faith in me; it refreshens without weakening and soothes without irritating. I often call it the rejuvenator.

Jean-Anthelme Brillat-Savarin (1755-1826) – *The Physiology of Taste*

DATE, ORANGE AND MINT SALAD WITH ORANGE GRANITA

Neil Perry – Rockpool, Sydney

32 fresh dates, soaked in hot water for 10 minutes, skins removed, halved and seeded

8 oranges, peeled and pith removed, segmented

16 mint leaves, thinly sliced

ORANGE GRANITA

1.8 litres freshly squeezed orange juice [about 15 oranges]

440 g [2 cups] caster sugar

1 For orange granita, strain orange juice through a fine sieve into a large bowl, add sugar and stir for 3 minutes or until sugar dissolves. Strain again through a fine sieve into a 23cm cake pan. Freeze mixture for 4 hours, stirring with a fork every 30 minutes to break up ice crystals, until mixture is frozen but still loose.

2 Place dates, oranges and mint in a bowl and combine gently, then divide date mixture among 300ml glasses, top with spoonfuls of granita and serve immediately.

Serves 8-10

CHERRIES IN BALSAMIC SYRUP WITH
WHIPPED RICOTTA AND LEMON CRISPS

CHERRIES IN BALSAMIC SYRUP WITH WHIPPED RICOTTA AND LEMON CRISPS

125 ml red wine

110 g [½ cup] caster sugar

1 tbsp balsamic vinegar

600 g cherries, pitted

2 tsp grated lemon rind

2 tbsp caster sugar, extra

2 sheets of filo pastry, halved

20 g butter, melted

500 g fresh ricotta

2 tbsp icing sugar

1 Place wine in a small frying pan and simmer over medium heat until reduced by two-thirds. Add caster sugar and ¼ cup water, stir over low heat until sugar dissolves, then bring to the boil and simmer without stirring until mixture forms a caramel. Remove from heat and add balsamic vinegar and ¼ cup water [taking care, as mixture will spit], then return to heat and stir until smooth. Pour syrup over cherries in a heatproof bowl and cool to room temperature.

2 Combine half the lemon rind and extra sugar. Brush pastry halves with melted butter and sprinkle with sugar mixture, then stack. Cut pastry into 8 strips lengthways, then in half widthways. Place strips on an oven tray and bake at 180C for 5 minutes or until crisp.

3 Using an electric mixer, beat ricotta, icing sugar and remaining lemon rind until light and fluffy. Divide whipped ricotta among 8 bowls, top with cherries and balsamic syrup and serve with lemon crisps to the side.

Serves 8

RAMBUTAN, RASPBERRY AND COCONUT SALAD WITH GINGER WINE SYRUP

250 ml Stone's Green Ginger Wine

2 tbsp caster sugar

500 g rambutans, peeled

120 g raspberries

50 g [½ cup] shaved fresh coconut, about ¼ coconut [see Glossary]

1 Place wine, sugar and ½ cup water in a small saucepan and stir over low heat until sugar dissolves. Boil syrup for 8-10 minutes or until reduced by half. Cool.

2 Place rambutans and ginger wine syrup in a bowl, combine well and refrigerate for 1 hour. Divide rambutans and syrup among 4 bowls, scatter with raspberries, top with a little shaved coconut and serve immediately.

Serves 4

salad equipment

MANDOLIN [1]

The classic tool for rapidly slicing vegetables and other firm foods into slices of consistent thickness, by running them back and forth over a sharp blade set at the appropriate height. There are cheap plastic versions of limited versatility, and some of these are quite effective, but the best are those used by professionals, made from heavy-gauge, nickel-plated steel with high-carbon steel blades and levers for adjusting to make plain or ripple slices from paper-thin to thick enough for chips, plus julienne strips and waffled slices. You hold the food down with a knob, so that your fingers are protected. It can seem complicated until you get used to it, and quite costly, but well worth it for serious cooks.

OLIVE WOOD SALAD BOWL [2]

Olive wood is extremely dense and hard. Oil an olive wood salad bowl before you use it, and thereafter, rinse it with warm water and dry thoroughly after each use. The oil in the salad dressings will gradually darken it and give it a soft gleam. If it ever looks dull, oil your hands and give it a good rub. Never rub the bowl with garlic as the smell will become stale.

SALAD HANDS [3]

With these squat wooden tools, you can toss a salad as gently and thoroughly as if you were using your own hands.

SALAD SPOONS [4]

Two spoons, or a spoon and wide fork, will pick up salad more neatly than one. They should be the right size to take a moderate portion at a time, and well balanced so that they will sit in the bowl without falling out. They need not be especially for salad – two tablespoons will do perfectly well. If the salad is arranged flat on a platter, a spatula and a fork will work best.

SMALL WIRE WHISK [5]

The best tool for turning oil and vinegar speedily into a smooth emulsion. Be sure you have a bowl small enough to go with it, as you will seldom need more than a few spoonfuls of dressing.

WIDE VEGETABLE PEELER [6]

You use the handle to pull this peeler directly towards you, so that it will run the entire length of the vegetable in a straight line – perfect for making tidy vegetable ribbons as well as peeling quickly and comfortably.

BOTTLES AND ACCESSORIES

If you want to dress your salad at the table, you will need glass or ceramic bottles or jugs for the oil and vinegar. Stoppered bottles are classic, but failing these, plain, workaday ones are usually best.

MORTAR AND PESTLE

Despite the wonders of electric food processors and spice mills, serious cooks of Asian or Middle Eastern food will want to grind spices and fresh ingredients by hand for the freshest and best results. Be sure your mortar is heavy enough to withstand vigorous pounding, and that the pestle fits both the mortar and your hand comfortably.

SCREW-TOP JARS

Easily the best choice for keeping ingredients fresh and airtight.

GLOSSARY

ANTIPASTO meaning before the meal. A selection of hot or cold appetisers.

BANANA BLOSSOMS the young flowers of banana trees, used in Sri Lankan, South-East Asian and Filipino cuisine, in soups and salads. Available from Asian food stores and select greengrocers. See page 94.

BARBERRIES native to most of Europe, the barberry has elongated bright red berries which, because of their high acidity, are rarely eaten raw. Ripe barberries are used in pies, preserves and syrups; they can also be candied. Available from Middle Eastern food stores.

BLOOD SAUSAGE also known as blood pudding or black pudding. A large link sausage, most commonly with a filling of pig's blood, suet, breadcrumbs and oatmeal. It is usually sold precooked.

BONITO FLAKES also known as kezuri-bushi. The bonito fish is a relative of the mackerel and tuna. The filleted fish is dried rock hard and shaved into pale pink, strongly aromatic flakes and used to make dashi and as a garnish. The larger flakes generally provide more flavour. Available from Asian food stores. See page 94.

BUFFALO MOZZARELLA soft, spun-curd cheese; originated in southern Italy where it is traditionally made from pure buffalo's milk.

BURGHUL (cracked wheat) hulled steamed wheat kernels that, once dried, are crushed into various size grains. Used in Middle Eastern dishes such as kibbeh and tabbouleh. See page 74.

CAPER FLOWERS are the flowers of the caper bush, salted and preserved in oil. The resulting flavour is more delicate than other caper products – capers (the buds) and caperberries (the fruit). They are used throughout the Mediterranean in many salad, fish and meat dishes and as an accompaniment with other vegetables. Available from specialty food stores.

CARPACCIO an Italian dish of slices or shavings of raw meat, such as beef fillet.

CASSIA is a dark, reddish-brown coloured spice available in quills and in ground form. It is derived from the bark of the cinnamon cassia tree and has a similar taste to cinnamon. Its slightly bittersweet flavour makes an intriguing addition to both sweet and savoury dishes. Available from spice shops and Asian food stores.

CAUL FAT also known as crépinette or omentum, is the lining from the pig's stomach. It is useful for keeping meats moist and, in the case of a sausage mixture, keeping it intact. Needs to be ordered in advance from the butcher.

CHESTNUTS have a sweet and nutty flavour and have been part of the staple diet of Southern Europe, Turkey and Asia for centuries. Cooked chestnuts are packaged in a variety of ways, including vacuum-packed in jars and cans without liquid and frozen. Available from specialty food stores and delicatessens.

CHILLI
Aleppo pepper moderately hot red chilli, also known as halaby pepper, that originates in Turkey and the Mediterranean coastal areas of the Middle East. It is sold sun-dried, seeded and crushed. Substitute with a mixture of cayenne and crushed chilli.
Ancho a broad, dried chilli with a reddish brown colour. Ranges from mild to hot and is one of the sweetest dried chillies. In its fresh state referred to as poblano chilli.
Birdseye the most commonly used fresh chillies in Thai cuisine, sometimes called bird peppers. These tiny, fiery chillies are red, green, lime or orange, depending on the variety. Dried birdseyes should not be used in place of the fresh ones; if necessary, substitute another fresh chilli.
Jalapeño (pronounced hal-uh-pen-yah) thick-fleshed green chillies with strong flavour and heat. The jalapeño is a popular chilli in Mexican cuisine and is often stuffed. Ripe, they can be dark green or red.
Roasted chilli powder available from Asian food stores.
Serrano a small, slightly pointed chilli with a hot, savoury flavour. The smooth, bright-green skin of the young serrano turns scarlet red then yellow as it matures. They are available fresh, canned, pickled and packed in oil (sometimes accompanied by vegetables), as well as dried and powdered.

COCONUT fresh coconuts are available from Asian greengrocers and other select greengrocers; the flesh should be soft, gelatinous and almost translucent. To shave the flesh, use a vegetable peeler or a large sharp knife.

COCONUT VINEGAR is low in acidity, with a musty flavour and a unique aftertaste. It is used traditionally in Asian and Thai dishes.

CORNICHON the French word for 'gherkin'. Smaller sour gherkins (3-4cm) are sold under this name.

COTECHINO SAUSAGE a specialty of Italy's Emilian provinces, this sausage is made from pork and is usually seasoned with nutmeg, cloves, salt and pepper.

DRIED SHRIMP these small sun-dried prawns are soaked in hot water or pounded to a paste before using. Available from Asian food stores. See page 94.

DUTCH-PROCESS COCOA 'dutching' is a method of alkalising cocoa. An alkali is added during processing, neutralising the astringent quality of the cocoa and giving it a rich, dark colour and smoother flavour. Available from specialty stores.

ELDERFLOWERS flowers of the elderberry tree. Available from select greengrocers, make sure to purchase unsprayed flowers. The tea is made from dried elderflowers and is available from specialist tea stores.

FARRO a variety of ancient wheat commonly used in parts of Italy.

FRENCH-TRIMMED bone ends cleaned of meat: cutlets, chicken drumsticks.

FRIED TOFU PUFFS packaged pieces (puffs or balls) of soft bean curd which have been deep-fried until the surface is brown and crusty and the inside almost dry. Available from Asian food stores.

FRITTATA Italian omelette cooked until the bottom is set, then inverted into another pan or placed under a grill to cook the top. The eggs may be mixed with herbs, diced cheeses, vegetables, seafood or meats. It can be eaten hot or cold.

GALANGAL a rhizome resembling ginger in shape but with a pink-hued skin. The flesh is more dense and fibrous than ginger, while the flavour is more delicate. Chop finely or slice thinly before use. Available from Asian food stores. See page 94.

GOAT'S MILK FETA goat's milk is the traditional base for this salty, crumbly cheese, giving the cheese a more complex taste. It is often stored in brine; if so, rinse it before using to remove some of the saltiness.

GREEN ONION sometimes known as shallot (UK) or scallion (USA); an immature onion pulled when the top is green, before the bulb has formed. Sold by the bunch.

GREEN PAPAYA is unripe papaya. Varying in length and shape, it is used in Thai cuisines raw and cooked. See page 94.

GREEN TEA SOBA NOODLES also known as chasoba. Japanese noodles made from both buckwheat and regular wheat flour, and flavoured with powdered green tea.

GROUND MACE this spice tastes and smells like a pungent version of nutmeg. Used to flavour sweet and savoury foods.

HARISSA fiery paste from North Africa, usually made from chillies, garlic, olive oil and caraway seeds. Refrigerate for up to two months, covered in a layer of oil to help preserve it. See page 74.

ITALIAN PEARL BARLEY smaller, whiter and quicker to cook than regular barley. Substitute pearl barley, but you will need to cook it for 45 minutes.

JAPANESE RICE SEASONING a mix of chopped nori, sesame seeds, caster sugar, sansho pepper and sea salt, available from Japanese and Asian food stores. To make your own, place 2 sheets of finely chopped nori, ⅓ cup sesame seeds, 3 tsp caster sugar, 1 tsp ground sansho pepper and 1 tbsp sea salt in a mortar and, using a pestle, grind to a coarse powder.

JAPANESE RICE VINEGAR colourless vinegar made from fermented rice and seasoned with sugar and salt. Also known as seasoned rice vinegar.

JICAMA (yam bean) this large, bulbous root vegetable has a thin brown skin and white crunchy flesh. Its sweet, nutty flavour is good both raw and cooked. See page 94.

JULIENNE technique of cutting vegetables, fruit or citrus rinds into 40mm-long strips approximately 3mm thick.

KAFFIR LIME LEAVES two glossy dark-green leaves joined end to end; used fresh or dried in many Asian dishes in the same manner as bay leaves or curry leaves, especially in Thai cooking. Sold fresh, dried or frozen; dried leaves are less potent so double the number called for in a recipe if using instead of fresh leaves. See page 94.

LABNA is a thick strained yoghurt with the consistency of thick sour cream and a mildly acidic taste. It is available from some supermarkets and Middle Eastern food stores. To make your own, place thick Greek-style yoghurt in a muslin-lined sieve over a bowl and refrigerate overnight.

LEBANESE EGGPLANT also known as Japanese eggplant. A long, slender variety of baby eggplant (aubergine), usually pale to dark purple in colour.

LOTUS STEMS, PICKLED also known as pickled lotus roots. The underwater root of the lotus plant is a rhizome growing in a string of links which, when peeled and sliced widthways, reveal creamy, firm flesh and holes that form a distinctive 'wheel' pattern. The sliced cooked roots are available in the refrigerator section of Asian food stores, while the younger, narrower type, labelled as pickled lotus roots or stems, are sold in jars of brine.

MARJORAM the most widely available is sweet marjoram. It can be used to flavour a variety of foods, particularly meats such as lamb and veal, and vegetables.

MIRIN sweet rice wine, used only in cooking. Found in Asian food stores. Substitute sweet sherry.

MISO, RED is dark brown in colour. A paste made in Japan from cooked, mashed, salted and fermented soy beans. It is a common ingredient in soups, sauces and dressings.

MIZUNA feathery, delicate salad green often found in mesclun

MOGHRABIEH sometimes called pearl couscous because of its size, is a large couscous made from semolina and is available from Middle Eastern and specialty food stores.

MUSCAT an aged, sweet fortified wine.

MUSHROOMS
Dried porcini dried form of an Italian mushroom, also known as a cep or boletus. Available from delicatessens. It must be rehydrated before use – soften in hot water for 20 minutes.
Enoki also called enokitake, it grows in clusters with long stems and small caps and has an unusually crunchy texture and almost fruity flavour.
Oyster also called shimeji in Japanese. Takes its name from its shape and greyish colour, with slight pepper overtones and a juicy texture.

Shiitake with a dark brown cap, this mushroom has a meaty flesh that is full-bodied. Its stems are tough and are removed but they add great flavour to stocks and sauces.

Swiss brown full-flavoured mushroom, also known as roman or cremini. If unavailable, substitute button or cap variety.

NORI paper-thin sheets of dried seaweed, ranging in colour from dark green to black. Nori has a sweet ocean taste and is generally used for wrapping sushi and rice balls however, when finely cut, it serves as a seasoning or garnish.

OLIVES

Gordal also known as the Queen Olive and the Sevillano, is a firm, plump green olive. Because of its large size, the Gordal is a favourite before the meal, especially when served with cocktails.

Ligurian black, small and high in oil, with a delicate sweet flavour. For more information see page 241.

Sicilian green vibrant green, large, fleshy olives prepared in the traditional Sicilian manner, using water and Mediterranean sea salt, giving them a subtle, buttery olive flavour and meaty texture. They contain no artificial ingredients or preservatives and must be refrigerated and used within a few days of purchase.

ORTIZ ANCHOVIES fished from the seas off northern Spain, only the largest grade of anchovy is preserved whole in rock salt and cured for four months, resulting in plump meaty fillets. Trimmed and filleted by hand, the hairy texture of lesser grade anchovies is eliminated.

ORZO tiny, rice-shaped pasta ideal for soups.

PALM SUGAR dark and light palm sugar is made from the sap of the sugar palm tree. Dark palm sugar is also known as nam tan pip, jaggery, jawa or gula melaka. It is usually sold in rock-hard cakes; the sugar is shaved off the cake with a sharp knife. Widely used in South-East Asian cuisine in sweet and savoury dishes.

PANCETTA an Italian bacon that is cured with salt and spices but not smoked. Available in both round and flat shapes.

PANKO coarse, dried Japanese breadcrumbs which give a crisp coating to fried foods. Available from Asian food stores; substitute day-old breadcrumbs.

PAPRIKA common name of a range of bright red powders made from a variety of sweet red capsicum. There are many types and grades, including smoked, hot, mild and sweet.

PASSATA sieved, puréed tomato, available in bottles from supermarkets and delicatessens.

PECORINO a dry, sharp, salty, Italian sheep's milk cheese.

PIN BONE method of removing small bones from fish fillets, using tweezers.

PINENUT derived from the pine cones of several varieties of pine trees. Generally to harvest the nuts, the cones must be heated. This labour-intensive process is the reason pinenuts are expensive. There are two main varieties. The Mediterranean or Italian nut is torpedo-shaped, has a light, delicate flavour and is the more expensive of the two. The Chinese pinenut is more triangular and it has a pungent flavour. Because of their high fat content, these nuts become rancid easily. Store in an airtight container in the refrigerator for no more than three months or freeze for up to nine months.

POLENTA yellow or white coarse granular meal made from maize or corn.

POMEGRANATE MOLASSES made from the juice of pomegranate seeds boiled down to a thick syrup. Available from select delicatessens and grocers, and Middle Eastern food stores. See page 74.

POMELO an ancestor of grapefruit, whose flavour it somewhat resembles. This largest of all citrus fruits is thick-skinned and sometimes slightly dry. See page 94.

PRAWN CRACKERS (krukup) a large, elongated prawn cracker popular in Indonesia and Malaysia. Bought in dried form, they are made from tapioca flour, prawns, salt and sugar. When deep fried they swell and become crisp.

PRESERVED LEMONS lemons preserved in salt and lemon juice. A common ingredient in North African cooking, available from specialty food stores and select greengrocers. See page 74.

PROSECCO a white wine grape that is grown primarily in the eastern part of Italy's Veneto region. Prosecco is made into light sparkling, full sparkling and still wines. The wines are crisp and appley and, though they can be sweet, are more often dry.

PROVOLONE PICCANTE this semi-hard stretched curd cheese is made from cow's milk and comes from Lombardy, Italy. Made in various shapes and sizes, the most common is a cylindrical or pear shape. They are bound with rope and have a bright yellow waxy rind. Younger cheeses are smaller, sweeter and mild flavoured, whereas larger cheeses are matured for at least two years and have a strong flavour.

PULLET EGGS the small eggs of a young hen. Available from supermarkets, sold as eggs for children.

QUARK a fresh, soft cheese made from skim milk, with a mildly sour taste.

QUINOA (pronounced keen-wa) an ancient grain from South America that is available from health food stores.

RAS EL HANOUT means 'head of the shop'. A traditional blend of Moroccan spices, showcasing the best spices a merchant might have for sale. It can include paprika, cumin, ginger, orris root, saffron, dried flowers, ginger, turmeric, fennel and bay leaf. See page 74.

ROSEWATER a distillation of rose petals that retains the intense fragrance and flavour of fresh roses. Rose water has been used for centuries in Eastern countries. Available from select grocers. See page 74.

SAFFRON THREADS dried stigmas from the crocus flower. Saffron is the world's most expensive spice because each flower produces only three stigmas, which must be hand-picked and delicately dried. It takes thousands of the tiny stigmas to make up a gram of saffron. Sometimes sold in powdered form, though it does not have the same intensity of flavour. Threads are available from specialty food stores and select delicatessens.

SAKE yellow Japanese rice wine made from fermented rice. It can be drunk hot or cold, or used in cooking, particularly in sauces and marinades.

SHALLOTS
French also known as eschalots. Small teardrop-shaped, golden brown bulbs that grow in clusters.
Fried usually served as condiments on the Thai table or sprinkled over just-cooked dishes. Available at Asian food stores. You can make your own by frying thinly sliced peeled red shallots until golden and crisp. They keep for months, if stored tightly sealed.
Red Asian small shallots with red skins, they are drier and more strongly flavoured than European shallots. Available from Asian food stores. See page 94.

SHRIMP PASTE also known as kapi, trasi or belacan; a strong-scented, very firm preserved paste made from salted, dried shrimp. Chop or slice thinly, then wrap in foil and roast before using. See page 94.

SNAKE BEANS long (about 40cm), round green beans, Asian in origin, with a taste similar to green or French beans. Often used in stir-fries, they are also called yard-long beans because of their length.

SOPRESSA a salami made from coarsely ground lean and fatty meat, typically cured for a year. Local to the Veneto region of Italy.

STAR ANISE a dried star-shaped pod that has an astringent aniseed taste; used to flavour stocks and marinades.

SUGAR, MUSCOVADO a very dark brown sugar which has a strong molasses flavour. The crystals are slightly coarser and stickier in texture than brown sugar.

SUMAC ground spice from a slightly astringent red berry. Available from spice shops. See page 74.

TAHINI sesame seed paste available from Middle Eastern food stores; most often used in hummus, baba ghanoush and other Lebanese recipes. See page 74.

TAMARIND PULP dried pulp of tamarind pods, sold in block form, needs to be soaked in hot water, then strained; the resulting liquid, not the tamarind pulp, is used in recipes. Available from Asian food stores.

TAMARIND PUREE also known as concentrate or paste. The commercial result of the distillation of tamarind juice into a condensed, compacted paste. Thick and purple-black, it is ready to use, with no soaking or straining required; can be diluted with water according to taste. Use to add zing to sauces, chutneys, curries and marinades. See page 94.

TAQUITO a small corn tortilla filled with cheese, ground or shredded meat, seafood, beans or cooked or raw vegetables, then rolled into a log shape. The narrow rolls can be served in snack-sized pieces or as an accompaniment to salads.

THAI BASIL also known as bai horapha, this is different from holy basil and sweet basil in appearance and taste. With smaller leaves and purplish stems, it has a slightly aniseed taste and is a typical flavour in Thai cuisine. See page 94.

TRUFFLE the fruiting body of a family of fungi that grow underground. A sliver of truffle infuses foods with an earthy aroma and flavour. The labour intensive method of harvest (dogs and pigs are trained to sniff them out) makes them expensive.

TURMERIC, FRESH also known as kamin, is a rhizome related to galangal and ginger. It must be grated or pounded to release its somewhat acrid aroma and pungent flavour.

VERJUICE unfermented grape juice, with a delicate lemon-vinegar flavour. Available from delicatessens. See page 144.

VIETNAMESE MINT a pungent and peppery narrow-leafed member of the buckwheat family, not the mint family. Also known as Cambodian mint, phak phai or laksa leaf, it is a common ingredient in Thai and Vietnamese cooking. See page 94.

VINCOTTO is made by cooking freshly crushed grapes until syrupy. It has a wonderful deep raisiny flavour, infused with orange. Available from delicatessens.

WASABI POWDER bright-green powder made from dried and ground wasabi, a Japanese rhizome related to horseradish. Available from Asian food stores.

WATER CELERY also known as Chinese celery and selom. Different from western celery as leaves are smaller, stems are narrower and the flavour more delicate. Available from Vietnamese greengrocers.

WHITE BALSAMIC CONDIMENT also known as white balsamic vinegar and white balsamic dressing. A combination of white wine vinegar and grape juice. See page 15.

ZA'ATAR a Middle Eastern spice mixture, comprising equal quantities of sesame seeds, thyme and sumac with a little salt. Sprinkled over meats and vegetables mixed with oil and used as a spread on bread. See page 74.

INDEX

CONVERSION CHART

MEASURES

One Australian metric measuring cup holds approximately 250ml, one Australian metric tablespoon holds 20ml, one Australian metric teaspoon holds 5ml. The difference between one country's measuring cups and another's is within a two- or three-teaspoon variance. North America, New Zealand and the United Kingdom use a 15ml tablespoon.

All cup and spoon measurements are level.

We use large eggs with an average weight of 60g.

Unless specified, all fruit and vegetables are medium sized and herbs are fresh.

DRY MEASURES

metric	imperial
15g	½oz
30g	1oz
60g	2oz
90g	3oz
125g	4oz (¼lb)
155g	5oz
185g	6oz
220g	7oz
250g	8oz (½lb)
280g	9oz
315g	10oz
345g	11oz
375g	12oz (¾lb)
410g	13oz
440g	14oz
470g	15oz
500g	16oz (1lb)
750g	24oz (1½lb)
1kg	32oz (2lb)

LIQUID MEASURES

metric	imperial
30ml	1 fluid oz
60ml	2 fluid oz
100ml	3 fluid oz
125ml	4 fluid oz
150ml	5 fluid oz (¼ pint/1 gill)
190ml	6 fluid oz
250ml	8 fluid oz
300ml	10 fluid oz (½ pint)
500ml	16 fluid oz
600ml	20 fluid oz (1 pint)
1000ml (1 litre)	1¾ pints

LENGTH MEASURES

metric	imperial
3mm	⅛in
6mm	¼in
1cm	½in
2cm	¾in
2.5cm	1in
5cm	2in
6cm	2½in
8cm	3in
10cm	4in
13cm	5in
15cm	6in
18cm	7in
20cm	8in
23cm	9in
25cm	10in
28cm	11in
30cm	12in (1ft)

OVEN TEMPERATURES

These oven temperatures are only a guide. Always check the manufacturer's manual.

	°C (Celsius)	°F (Fahrenheit)	Gas Mark
Very slow	120	250	½
Slow	150	275-300	1-2
Moderately slow	160	325	3
Moderate	180	350-375	4-5
Moderately hot	200	400	6
Hot	220	425-450	7-8
Very hot	240	475	9